Life with the Boys

One Woman's Life in Chemistry

~

PHYLLIS R. BROWN

Life with the Boys, Published December 2016

Editorial and proofreading services: Jenna Lloyd, Kathy Bruins, Karen Grennan

Interior layout and cover design: Howard Johnson

Photo credit, Front cover: Variety of colors background, ID: 843572, designed by Freepik.com

SDP Publishing

Published by SDP Publishing, an imprint of SDP Publishing Solutions, LLC.

For more information about this book contact Lisa Akoury-Ross by email at lross@SDPPublishing.com.

ISBN-13 (print): 978-0-9977224-9-9

e-ISBN-13 (ebook): 978-0-9981277-0-5

Library of Congress Control Number: 2016953809

© 2016, Phyllis R. Brown

Printed in the United States of America

To Dr. John Edwards and Ruth Edwards.

To my accomplished and accomplishing grandchildren: Emily Fialky, Garrett Brown, Pamela Brown, Zachary Brown, Molly Donovan, Ezra Pryor, Daniel Groveman, Rebecca Groveman, and Arianna Groveman.

To women everywhere daring to dream and motivated to achieve.

Acknowledgments

To Susan Lougee who lent her counsel, editing, and organizational skills.

To my children, daughters and sons by marriage, grandchildren and great grandchildren, for inspiring me to share my story with them and to document my professional life as fully as possible.

To Lisa Akoury-Ross and Jenna Lloyd of SDP Publishing Solutions for their expertise and professional guidance, their commitment to my story, and to me personally.

To My Laurelmead family, particularly Ron Bruno, Sue Vartian, John Goncalves, and Roseanne Moffitt. They, along with every member of the community, show what kindness, respect and mutual caring can bring to each of us.

To my friends, those from early childhood to those we forged together as we met as adults. I cannot adequately express my appreciation for their support, all we've shared and added to one another's lives.

To my URI family Sue Geldart, Sze Yang, Dave Freeman and Christina Robb especially, as well as other fellow faculty members, and former graduate students; I loved our work together. And to those gifted administrators such as Winnie Brown (no relation), so instrumental in achieving our mission of science education.

To my artist daughter, Judith Brassard Brown, who spent many hours discussing and working on this project with me.

And last but not least, this book is another part of my life with Bert, the love we had for each other, and the pride we shared for each other's accomplishments.

Contents

Introduction

I opened the door to the convention hall at the University of Rhode Island (URI) and walked into my past. A burly, bearded man approached and swooped me up.

"Phyllis," he cried, "It's so good to see you. You look great; haven't changed a bit."

That was a lie or at least a gross exaggeration with the best of intentions. We had not seen each other in over ten years. Memories of my past life, my years as a scientist came flooding back. I had been a chemist for over thirty years and a successful one at that . . . unbelievable. As I looked around, it was déjà vu. So few women present. Like before, it was *life with the boys.*

CHAPTER 1

In the Beginning

~

The URI student's hand shot up before I had even opened the Q&A portion of my "Women in Science" presentation. "Why did you decide to become a scientist?" she asked.

Quick as a flash I answered, "It was the only job in which my father could not control me." At that very moment, the real reason that I became a chemist sprung into my mind. My father did not understand the sciences at all, so he could not tell me what to do. I wanted to be my own person.

Although his father had put aside money to pay for college, when my father finished high school, he used that money to open a peddling business—selling candy. Making money was his objective because of the hardships he experienced growing up during the Depression. After years of financial struggles, my father became a well-respected candy manufacturer known as "the Lollipop King."

Strong and controlling, my father became a successful, self-made businessman. It was his way or the highway. Growing up, I learned not to make waves. Nevertheless, as a young and feisty woman, just as smart and strong as he, I wanted to live my own life. I wanted out from under his thumb. When I told him I wanted to go to Simmons College in Boston, he thought it was a fine idea.

"You will then have a career. In case anything happens to your husband, you will be able to support yourself."

Because of the Depression, he worried about my ability to provide for myself. He did not want his daughters working in a five-and-dime store (Woolworth or Kresge in those days), earning the lowest pay, and being at the bottom of the prestige scale. Such was the fate of women with no skills when they had to support themselves. At that time I did not have a boyfriend, much less a husband!

Thus began my long and checkered career, one that I never planned or plotted. I just went with the flow and ended up having not only a very successful career as a chemist, but also a wonderful husband, four incredible children, subsequent grandchildren, and even great-grandchildren. Choosing a special man was key to my success in raising four remarkable children.

Overweight as a child, I did not thin out until I was twelve or thirteen. But those years of being a hefty youngster left an indelible mark on my psyche. Although for the rest of my life I was relatively thin and worked to keep my weight under control, I labeled myself a plain, overweight girl.

Regardless of my size, I had close friends, loved to read, was very active in school, and saw most everything through rose-colored glasses. I enjoyed all kinds of activities with friends or family including playing tennis, riding my bike, and ice skating at York's Pond. I cherished our summers at Barrington Beach in Rhode Island, even though I hated the seaweed that often covered much of the sand. There, I had a gang of friends, mostly boys, that I hung out with climbing trees, playing cards, swimming, and wandering the area on our bikes.

My parents were content to let me do whatever I wanted as long as I was home for dinner and dressed appropriately. As a middle child, I learned how to do whatever I wanted—within the confines of the rules of time. I particularly liked hanging with my next-door neighbor,

Stanley. I delighted in spending time at his house and enjoyed sharing the fresh, homemade root beer and ripe watermelon his family would dive into, rather than eat politely with a knife and fork.

Not popular among the group of petite classmates in high school, I blossomed early and always seemed to appeal to the older boys. At a young age I accepted myself as I was and grew up unscarred by this. Bert, who I had known my entire life and would become my husband, was the first one to tell me I was beautiful. Through the ups and downs of our sixty-five years together, he never wavered on that thought.

I liked school. When I had homework, I always saved the best for last: arithmetic. Solving math problems was fun for me. In high school I took a full load of challenging classes and still made time to work on the school newspaper, the yearbook, and manage the debate team. Never one to sit still, I took violin lessons after school and played in the high school orchestra. I knew early on that I would never be a musician, but I loved music—especially playing in the orchestra. In fact, while in a violin lesson in 1938, the Great New England Hurricane hit Providence and destroyed almost nine thousand homes. The wind howled and trees toppled, but I fiddled away, oblivious to Mother Nature's destruction outside.

When I graduated high school in 1940, I applied to only two colleges: Pembroke College, which was the women's college of Brown University (Brown) in Providence, and Simmons College in Boston. I preferred Simmons to Pembroke. I wanted to escape Providence even though I was only sixteen. In elementary school, I had advanced ahead three separate semesters and graduated more than a year early.

Looking back, I knew my father would exert too much influence if I lived at home for college. Moreover, while my mother did not openly support me going away to college, I knew she loved my determination to pursue my dreams. Ironically, I was as stubborn and determined as my father. We were very much alike with one exception. While I was a serious student, he never cared about academics. My father saw school as a waste of time although he pursued business with the same thirst I had for my studies. He persuaded my grandfather to let him use that college money to start a business because my father was driven to succeed. He worked hard to become successful in America in a way his immigrant parents never did. Our entire family's financial stability rested on his shoulders, as his company became the fulcrum.

My sights were set on a different path. While anxious to get on with my life, I wanted far more from my education than finding a suitable man to marry. Simmons would bring more freedom for me in Boston, as I could figure out who I was and wanted to be. Simmons was dedicated to educating women in a variety of professions.

At first, my father thought he could not afford to send me to Simmons. At Pembroke I could live at home, and he would save the cost of room and board. Since my sister was a senior at Simmons when I started, and it was still the Depression, I don't know how he managed paying for both of us. Somehow, he made it happen, and off I went—the most naïve sixteen-year-old ever. I loved being in Boston, Simmons, and my classes and classmates. Most of all, I loved being a college girl. I planned to play in the Simmons orchestra, but it was so small compared to our large high school orchestra that I put away my violin and never played again. There wasn't enough of a challenge for me in an orchestra with so few members.

Despite the tensions in the world, with Hitler walking all over Europe, the hints of something terrible happening with the European Jews, and the Depression, I was in love with life. The freedom of being away from home exhilarated me. I had only one small problem. At Simmons they were experimenting with advanced placement (AP) exams for selected students, and I took the AP chemistry exam. Unfortunately, I passed it. I had to skip freshman chemistry and start in an organic chemistry course with all sophomores. I was lost and frustrated! Organic chemistry involved memorizing a huge amount of material and I had no idea how to organize it. So I earned a D in my first hour-long exam. I had never failed an exam in my life. In fact, I had all As and here—in my proposed major no less—I had a D! I was devastated.

Fortunately, I knew a young man who was a teaching assistant in chemistry at nearby Northeastern University. I told him what happened and he rescued me. Over that Thanksgiving weekend, Bert tutored me so well that I never again had trouble with a chemistry course.

When I first went to Simmons in the fall of 1940, Bert and I started spending time together. I had known him my entire life in Providence, as my uncle's best friend, and he had given me a ride home here and there. However, in Boston it was different. Over that fall we started dating. Through casual, occasional evenings out every couple of weeks or so, I fell in love. Being with Bert differed from being on other dates; I was comfortable with him. I could be completely myself.

Most of our dates were low-key although we dated regularly. At least we did at first, until the time he brought me as his date to chaperone a Northeastern University sophomore dance. That's when he found out I was only sixteen. To say he was shocked that he had been dating a sixteen-year-old was putting it mildly. After all, I knew he was ten years older, even if he had conveniently forgotten the difference in our ages. Luckily, our relationship survived the shock, and we picked up where we had left off several weeks later.

We would go to nearby Norumbega Park, a well-known Massachusetts amusement park and entertainment venue that hosted big bands of the day. There, large crowds of college kids jitterbugged or swayed to the dreamy songs of Benny Goodman and Tommy Dorsey among others. In between dances we sat on loveseats and had drinks and nibbles. The low light of the hall was romantic, and those dates were the highlight of the year. At the end of the year, Bert took me to a Boston Pops Concert at Symphony Hall and treated me to cashew nuts, my favorite snack.

Bert had a very strict budget because of his modest salary as a teaching assistant. From it he had to cover his living expenses including a car, his courses at the Massachusetts Institute of Technology (MIT), and sending money home to help his mother. Although he wanted to finish his PhD, when the government implemented the draft in the spring of 1941, he received a very low draft number. Although he could defer his service because he was teaching chemistry, he enlisted in the Naval Reserves as an officer. By July, Bert was serving in the Navy.

The week before he left for duty, Bert asked me to spend the day with him at Narragansett Pier in Rhode Island. He first asked my mother's permission, and I was surprised when my mother said yes, since it would be a full day with a long drive there and back. I went, and we had a glorious day on the beach. I had never seen such an incredibly beautiful beach. After the stones and seaweed at Barrington Beach, this was heaven. We spent the whole day riding the waves, sunning, and walking the beach. Then Bert showed me around the small town of Narragansett, especially his old haunts; the places he had enjoyed when he worked there during his college summers. At the end of the day, I hated to say goodbye to him. I had no idea where the Navy would send him or when I would see him again.

When I went home to Barrington for the summer, my family lived as we had for many summers before. Although I could drive we were a one-car family, and my father needed the car. I biked each day to the post office to see if there was a letter for me. Because Bert was extremely busy in naval school the first month, I rarely heard from him. He finished at the top of the class and secured the best assignment. While the others went to naval stations all over the world, Bert was stationed at the headquarters of the Bureau of Ordnance (BuOrd) in the heart of Washington, DC. Once there he wrote me quite regularly. At that time BuOrd was responsible for the acquisition, storage, and deployment of all naval weapons. A decade or so later, BuOrd became a part of the Bureau of Naval Weapons.

In the fall of 1941, when I was back at Simmons, he had a chance to visit me when a friend who was an Air Force pilot had room for a passenger on a flight to Boston. The Harvard-Brown football game was in Cambridge that weekend. It was a glorious fall day, crisp and sunny, and Bert invited me to the game. He bought me a beautiful, large, yellow chrysanthemum to pin on my coat.

As we sat in the bleachers, I heard someone calling my name. Two rows behind us were my aunt and uncle—then living in Norwich, Connecticut—who were there with a group of friends. My uncle had played football for Brown in the early thirties and they were having a mini-reunion with some of his college classmates. My aunt was more than a little surprised to see me with her kid brother's best friend. I later heard that it made for some interesting dinner table conversation the following night.

Falling in love was so gradual; I do not know when it started. Was it on those early rides home to Providence in his car in the fall of 1940? Or did absence make the heart grow fonder in the summer of 1941? Regardless, I soon realized that I could not wait until the next visit with him. Certainly, all other dates paled in comparison to him. Was it his dashing appearance in a naval officer's uniform? I must admit the naval uniforms were the most appealing of any of the uniforms the young men were wearing.

By the beginning of 1942, I could not wait to see him, to hear his voice, or to receive a letter from him. Of all my friends in Providence and in Boston, I—the youngest—fell in love first. Bert really was the secret of my success. He was a feminist before anyone had heard the name Betty Friedan.

Life is so full of twists and turns! Bert, who grew up in Providence, could never have dated me if I had gone to Pembroke, with him being ten years older than I was and my uncle's best friend. In fact, he babysat my sister and me as youngsters. I was the kid niece, and he did not tell my uncle we were dating until after our engagement. I always liked him because he did not tease me like my uncle and his other friends did.

By then, I was grown up, and in Boston it was different. We were away from the prying eyes of family and friends. Bert had a car, and many weekends he came back to Providence. Several female college students, including my sister, hitched a ride with him to Providence on Saturday and back to Boston on Sunday. I quickly became a part of that group. I would find myself sitting in the front seat, next to Bert, and he always let me off last. I later learned I should have been dropped off first, but since I didn't know Boston, I didn't know the difference.

Because Simmons offered a degree in chemistry, it never occurred to me that I could not be a chemist. Simmons was a women's college started by businessman, John Simmons, in 1899 to train women to support themselves. It was divided into schools (e.g., science, home economics, business, English, nursing, etc.) and when you entered you had to declare your school. I immediately told my advisor science, knowing that the courses were demanding. Students were closely monitored, and the environment was nurturing yet professional. From our first day the administration admonished us to act, think, and dress like a professional. I do not know if Simmons is like that today. In addition to all the science and math courses, we had to take a rigorous English composition course, public speaking, and typing. The typing was to get your foot in the door for a job as a typist, in case you could not get a job in your field. I am eternally grateful to Simmons for preparing me for life in the real world.

I had a checkered career. I zigged, zagged, and did not go straight to a goal as men usually do. I graduated from college with a BS in chemistry, worked for a year, was a housewife for almost twenty years, went back to school for six years, and then taught and did research for over thirty years. One may think I did nothing for those twenty years that I stayed home. I once said to a young woman whom I had just met, "Do you work?"

She retorted, "Yes, I work and I work hard. I am raising three children and running a household."

Her point was well taken, having been in those shoes. After that I always asked a woman if she worked outside the home.

In those early years, although I did not work outside the home, I raised four children, was active in the community, had a full social life, and was (or tried to be) a good wife, mother, and daughter.

My path to a career in chemistry was a long and winding road. I did not have a set goal; it was serendipity. In the ninth grade we had to make a career book. I did mine on bacteriology, and I was greatly impressed with Antoine Van Leeuwenhoek who discovered "the little beasties" we now call bacteria. While I laugh to look back on it, I ended up becoming a chemist simply because I could not draw the bacteria I viewed through the microscope in my college freshman bacteriology course. Moreover, chemistry had a beauty, a rationale, and a structure that appealed to me. Therefore, I decided the world could use another chemist—me. However, in a conference with my English professor, she told me that if I wanted to change from science to English, she thought I would do well. I knew a career as an English teacher or librarian was not for me although the solid basis she gave me in English composition was immeasurably helpful to my success as a research chemist.

The fifth of December dawned bright and clear—a crisp winter day in 1941, which boded well for a visit from Bert. He had called a few days before and said he could get a ride up from Washington with an Air Force buddy who had room for a passenger.

"Am I available for a date? Of course," I said and quickly cancelled all other plans.

Since he arrived late Friday afternoon, I happily skipped German class and met him at the airport. I do not remember all that we did that weekend, but I do remember that I was falling for him. Early that Sunday afternoon, I tearfully said good-bye to him and settled in to catch up on studying for my Monday classes. Suddenly, I heard a big commotion in the hallway of my dorm. My door flew open and Evie, my next-door neighbor, burst in screaming, "Did you hear the news? The Japanese bombed Pearl Harbor! They may be bombing us! The President is going to speak. Turn on the radio!"

My first thoughts went to Bert. What did he know when he was here? Did he get back safely to Washington?

Later that night, I poured my heart out in a letter to Bert.

Darling, a couple of hours ago light dawned in this thick skull of mine, and I realized that we were at war. I can't believe it; it does not seem real. Since I heard the news that Japan declared war on the United States and Great Britain, I have not been able to study. In fact, I can't do anything but listen to the news.

Darling, I had not realized what being at war meant until I heard that one hundred American sailors were killed in Hawaii. (We later learned that it was over two thousand, not 100, who died at Pearl Harbor). It's so horrible to live when you know such sad history is being made. It seems so futile to go on studying seemingly unimportant details knowing that there is so much to be done. But of course, we all realize that the best we can do is to stay in school, get the most out of our studies, and when we are properly trained, take our place side-by-side with the rest of the men and women engaged in defending our country. This afternoon I did not comprehend the vastness of this horrible mess. Although I realized that war was inevitable, today is so much nearer home than some vague tomorrow.

Darling, I am so very happy that we had last night together, unmarred by any thoughts of unrest or fighting. I heard that all soldiers and sailors on leave were ordered back to their posts. I now know how wise you were last May to join the Naval Reserves.

Tonight has been the weirdest I've ever spent. We all realize, of course, how grave the situation is, and in the girl's dorm you can sense the tension. With brothers, sweethearts, and relatives in everything from the Air Corps to the Army, the air here is as anxious as any place.

It is so funny, dearest, to have traffic going outside my window as usual. It seems as though everything ordinary should stop and only preparations to beat Japan should go on. But, of course, that would be neither necessary nor wise. Life, I guess, must go on as usual but will take on a more serious and graver aspect. I think we here realize that our childhood is really over, and soon we must assume our responsibilities as adults. It's hard to get used to that idea because it hit us so suddenly.

You know, darling, I do not worry about the war itself but of the consequences of the outcome. No matter who wins, I am beginning to wonder if there'll be any civilization left at all. But I guess this isn't the time to think of that.

Goodnight darling, Phyllis

Bert's letters to me were like the anatomy of a love affair. It started in July with an occasional letter that opened with, *Dear Phyllis*, and ended with, *Yours, Bert.* In between, he described events of the day. As time went on, the letters were more regular, mostly every day. By the end of the summer, they started, *Phyllis dear*, and concluded with, *Love, Bert.* By January 1942 the letters began with, *Phyllis, dearest*, and usually concluded with declarations of love and longing that only young lovers felt.

My daughter, on reading them recently, said to me, "Mom, Dad wrote lovely love letters, but they certainly were tame."

In those days any mention of sex was unheard of. The world was so different back then. The nice thing about the early 40s, however, was that since there was no email and few phone calls, we wrote to each other, so a record of our romance lives on.

Some of the letters, however, contained more than just our romantic thoughts. In one letter I had apparently asked a question regarding a chemical problem, and Bert answered it in detail. In another he wrote me a love letter in Navy legalese, which was fun to read. After we became engaged, there were many details about the wedding or our apartment and, of course, acknowledgments of all the activities like bridal showers or parties. Whether his letters were long or short, I eagerly anticipated them and bawled him out if I went a few days without receiving a letter.

We had to settle for a long-distance courtship consisting of letters and occasional visits. On his visit in early March of 1942, with dinner at the centuries-old Durgin Park restaurant in Boston, Bert asked me when I would come back with him to Washington. I heard a proposal in his question. Bert teased me that as an honest woman, I had merely misunderstood. Even without a formal proposal, we decided to get married. The biggest obstacle was getting my parents to agree to their youngest daughter marrying at such a tender age.

It took the entire next weekend to convince them that we should get married so we could set the date. I firmly thought of myself as a competent adult at the ripe old age of eighteen and could not believe how stunned and shell-shocked my parents appeared. They had no idea

I had been seriously dating Bert. We had been seeing each other in Boston, so news had not yet reached them. If we had been dating in Providence, they would have known how serious we were about each other. Bert asked his brother, who was also an officer in the Naval Reserve—as well as an attorney—to be our advocate. He somehow convinced my parents to give their blessing. An engagement party was June 6, and the wedding was provisionally set for September 6, dependent upon confirmation of Bert's leave for that weekend.

Bert had proposed to me in the spring of my sophomore year, and back then you followed your sailor or soldier husband to wherever he was stationed, if possible. I have wondered if I would have married at eighteen had there been no war. I was young and in love, and it never occurred to me that I would not follow him wherever he went.

As we had hoped, Bert did get his leave. We were married at my parents' home on a beautiful day over Labor Day weekend in September 1942. An open house for all our family and friends followed the ceremony. We loved each other and we loved celebrating with everyone. Even walking down the aisle with my father whispering in my ear, "You can still change your mind. You don't have to get married. We can just have a great party," did not lessen my enjoyment of the day. As soon as Bert stepped on the glass, all present sighed, "Mazel tov!" and as we kissed to seal the bond, our new life began.

Although I loved Simmons and my life in Boston, I happily traded my life there for our life in Washington, DC. I transferred to George Washington University (GW), the university nearest to Bert's office. I had never been further from home than New York City, and other than my tiny dorm room, I definitely had never kept house. For whatever reason, it was not daunting, and looking back I am surprised that Bert did not worry about the ability of his eighteen-year-old bride to tackle the chores. It must have been love!

After our weeklong honeymoon in the Pocono Mountains, we settled into life in our small apartment in Kaywood Gardens in Mount Rainier, Maryland, a suburb of Washington. Our rent was sixty dollars per month—a far cry from today's rents.

Bert went back to work the day after we returned from our honeymoon, and I started school a week later. It was quite a shock trying to find my place at a large, sprawling university like GW, after the warm and intimate atmosphere of Simmons. I knew no one but quickly learned the ropes. It felt chaotic at the time being a small fish in a big pond. Many of the GW professors had left for wartime duties, but I survived, and the small group of chemistry majors soon became my friends. Because Bert had to be at work very early he dropped me off before eight in the morning. A few of us who arrived early would study in the only classroom open at that hour. There, I had the good fortune to become friends with Margaret Truman whose father, Harry, also dropped her off.

Bert and I marketed on weekends and watched our budget carefully. Since a large head of cabbage was very cheap, I learned to make every cabbage dish possible (and there were a lot). Finally, after I proudly served us another cabbage dish for dinner, Bert exploded. "No more! I have had enough cabbage. We have to watch our money but not to this extent."

So the cabbage run stopped. We started a ritual of attending the farmers' market on Saturday afternoons when it was closing, and all the farmers just wanted to get rid of the leftover produce. We were able to bring home a variety of fresh fruits and vegetables for little more than we had been spending on cabbage.

We had been married less than a month when my father called. He was coming to Washington on business and would be visiting us. I carefully planned dinner and went to the farmers' market to shop. At home I started to prepare the chicken I had purchased and much to my dismay, discovered that it was cleaned but not drawn. It still had all the innards left in. I frantically called Bert at the Navy Department. Luckily, as a boy he had seen his grandmother eviscerate a chicken, so step-by-step he patiently told me over the phone what to do. By the time Bert and my father arrived, I had prepared a tasty chicken dinner. I had wanted to please my father, show him I was grown up and could handle a household. I accomplished my goal.

During our three years in Washington, Bert and I had our ups and downs as most newlyweds do. I foolishly took six courses (including three lab courses) my first year at GW. Everything went fairly well until I came down with the measles and missed almost two weeks of school. What a disaster! I struggled making up all the labs and coursework, but somehow I made it. My mother was very upset with Bert for not telling her I was sick. She would have come to take care of me. I must admit, those days sick in bed and by myself were very long and lonely.

There were times when Bert worked ten- or twelve-hour days, six or seven days a week. I later learned that those were the periods when the United States prepared to invade the various Pacific Islands such as Iwo Jima or Okinawa. Since his responsibility included buying all the small arms ammunition, artillery ammunition, and demolition material for the Navy and the Marines, I could feel his tension. As a young wife eager to support her husband, I longed to know what was troubling him. I understood and came to accept that he could not talk about his job because it was classified.

After my first year at GW, Bert said, "Why don't you take the summer off and relax?"

That sounded good to me. I could sleep late and did not have to spend my nights and weekends studying. However, after a week alone in our small apartment, I began to go stir crazy. Finally, I had to do *something*, and I easily found a job for the summer at the National Institute of Health (NIH) in the toxicology section. My first real job! I did not know that it was the beginning of my long and unconventional career as a chemist. I learned a lot and felt good contributing to the war effort. My project of developing methods of desalinization of seawater was very important during the war. One day, however, I opened one of my instrument drawers and found it crawling with cockroaches! That was Washington, DC! Southern city living was different from how I grew up.

In addition, I was amazed that at 4:15 p.m. every afternoon the staff started to clean up and punch out for the day as close to four thirty as possible. Did everyone's experiments end so promptly? I was raised differently and taught to finish what I started. I never did understand their mindset. Unfortunately, I joined the mob because my carpool had to leave promptly too. Everyone had to be on time for the carpool. The summer ended, which meant the job was over, and it saddened me. It had been a good experience.

My senior year at GW was uneventful. Assisting in the freshman chemistry labs, I finished all the requirements to get a BS in chemistry. It was required that I take a qualifying exam in the optics part of physics, which was covered in the first year of physics at GW but in the second year at Simmons. Because of the move I never learned about optics, so Bert tutored me, and I passed with flying colors.

A couple of my classmates disappeared right after graduation, and we later learned they were recruited to work on the atomic bomb at the nuclear facility in Oak Ridge, Tennessee. After graduation from GW I found a job at the Geophysical Laboratory of the Carnegie Institute of Washington. In the spring the azaleas growing in front of the lab were dazzling. Here, there was teatime at three-thirty each afternoon. They served two types of cookies: the packaged kind that included sandwich cookies (like Oreos) and regular cookies. All the older scientists would argue over the sandwich cookies. I said to Bert, "Why don't the scientists just buy a package of Oreos and everyone would be happy?" I finally made that suggestion to the scientists, but it fell on deaf ears. I think they liked the challenge.

The lab was in the northwest region of Washington, DC, and Mount Rainier was in the northeast, making our commute difficult. Bert found us an apartment closer to work, and one hot day, we moved. Since apartments were at a premium in the Washington area, I am not sure how he maneuvered that one. The location was great, right off Connecticut Avenue, near Rock Creek Park and a nice strip shopping mall. We enjoyed all the amenities of the area, and I could walk to work or take a bus for the few blocks. In what little spare time we had, we bicycled and picnicked in the park, skated at an ice rink up the street, or swam in the pool at the Wardman Park Hotel down Connecticut Avenue.

We even canned peaches and tomatoes, which we bought by the bushel from the nearby market. There was no television then, but we listened on the radio when Franklin Roosevelt received the nomination for his fourth term as president. Harry Truman was on the ticket as vice president. We heard Roosevelt's inauguration address and sadly, soon after, watched his funeral cortege down Pennsylvania Ave. We also went to downtown Washington to celebrate the surrender of Germany in Europe and then in August the surrender of Japan after the explosion of the atomic bombs in Hiroshima and Nagasaki. These were heady times to be in Washington.

Until the war, the Geophysical Laboratory was a sleepy little place in which each scientist worked at his own pace on his individual research. I worked for a volcanologist who was studying gun erosion for the war effort. For the first time in his life, he had two assistants. Since he did not trust either one of us to work alone, he had no idea what to do with us. So when he worked with his other assistant, I could not work in the lab. When he worked with me, his other assistant could not do any work. And when he was carrying out his own experiments, neither of us could work. We both had to sit and do nothing. Those days were endless.

After about six months, I could not stand the long and tedious days. Being young and feisty, I came home one day and told Bert I was going to quit. I was going to tell off my boss and then tell his boss what a waste of my time and the government's money it was to be working there. All because our boss did not trust in our abilities. Bert listened to my ranting, sat me down, and told me that was not the right way to leave a job. Do not burn your bridges. Do what you have to so you leave on good terms. It took him until midnight to convince me to resign quietly. I never regretted his advice, and I learned a lesson that helped me later in my career and in my life.

I quickly found a contract job as a chemist at Harris Research Laboratory, a small research lab with government contracts. Additional contracts were available due to the war. I loved working with other young, lively chemists who also focused on getting their work done.

Our troops in the South Pacific were facing health issues because of mold, and the government urgently needed new treatments for tent canvas, so my project involved developing a better way to mildew-proof canvas. Helping the soldiers who were defending our country was fulfilling. Like most chemists we were not there to find out the results of our hard work.

As war came to an end, the lab not only offered me a permanent job but offered Bert a position as well. I would have loved to stay in Washington to help this young company grow, but Bert wanted to sort out the many different opportunities available to him. He was discharged from the Navy due to the first-in-first-out policy, and since he had joined before the war, he qualified to return to civilian life after Japan surrendered.

CHAPTER 2

The Little Housewife

~

Finally, the war ended, and we had to face the question, "What next?" I wanted Bert to go back to MIT on the GI bill and finish his work for a PhD. He only had one more year to go when he enlisted. His captain wanted him to stay in the Navy and offered him the possibility of a rapid promotion to commander. In addition, several of the companies he had worked with during those wartime years offered him very good jobs as a chemist. However, my father talked to him about starting a new business: manufacturing plastic containers for his candy company. Plastics was a new field, and the thought of his own business excited Bert. I really was not enthusiastic about going back to Providence or of Bert going into business—especially with my father. I preferred an academic life, but was overruled on both counts. Back we went to our hometown. The move disappointed me.

After the uncertainty of the war, most couples our age wanted to settle down and raise a family with the husbands starting a career. Our oldest son, Charlie, born in September 1946, came in the first wave of baby boomers. About a dozen of our friends all had babies in late 1946 or early 1947. We knew nothing at all about babies, but we learned quickly. In those days classes for parents didn't exist, and only a few books were available. The most famous ones were by Spock or Gesell. We learned about the stages of pregnancy and then the skills of parenting mostly from each other. During our pregnancies, the women met and walked to our favorite gathering spot, Wayland Square, where there were small shops and restaurants. Pregnant, we looked like a herd of elephants all walking together.

After the babies were born, we stopped traffic with our parade of strollers. Most of those babies later went to school together and have maintained their friendships even though they have scattered geographically. No play dates or organized classes existed as they do today and, of course, absolutely no househusbands. None of the women considered working outside the home. We worked hard as homemakers, since few of the appliances of today were available, and no one had help outside of an occasional babysitter. Because the men started in new jobs or careers, most of them worked long hours, and even if they wanted to help with the children, they did not have time. Bert was great with the kids, when he was home. Unlike many of the men of his era, he did not mind changing diapers or feeding the children. Many a time when Bert had to go to Springfield or Leominster on business, we would bundle the baby into the car and go along with him for the ride. For me it was a change of scenery, and it meant company for Bert.

Common interests made life with the girls fun. We compared notes on when our first-born stood, rolled over, or said his or her first word. Moreover, we reassured one another if a child took longer than the others did to reach a milestone. I remember teaching one friend how to take her newborn son's temperature. She worried he was sick and needed to tell the pediatrician if he had a temperature. We were a support group for each other.

As the children got older, our interests diverged. Some of us joined the PTA, and others were active in the League of Women Voters (LWV). We branched out from our small starter apartments to larger homes in which we could grow. A group of us bought or built homes in Pawtucket, a neighboring small city where the prices of homes and taxes were much lower than in Providence, the capital of Rhode Island. We worked to improve the schools and helped clean up the city, recognized in the late 30s as one of the most corrupt cities in America.

Our volunteer work trained us for the next phase of our lives, when our children went off to school all day. We were part of the first generation of women who went back to school, started a career, or plunged completely into volunteer work. A few, however, just wanted to play bridge, canasta, or mah jongg, while others used the freedom for sports or shopping. I was one of the lucky ones whose husband encouraged and supported my growth. I remember playing tennis with a friend when I told her I could not play the next week because I was going to a conference in Boston. Incredulously, she said, "Your husband is letting you go?" I could not believe this brilliant woman was not permitted to use her talents to the fullest. The revelation amazed me!

None of us had any money when starting our careers and families. The men lost three to four of their most productive career years because of the war. Despite the stresses and strains of new babies and civilian lives, we all bonded and found ways to enjoy life together.

Impossible to go out to dinner, we got together for homemade desserts and coffee, played penny ante, and shared many laughs. I will never forget the night I invited a group over for cake and coffee. I went to serve the beautiful, tall angel cake I made from scratch and found that my two little boys, two-and-a-half-year-old Ron and four-year-old Chuck, had scooped out the inside of the cake and left the shell standing. What an embarrassing moment! I made do serving the remnants of the cake. Everyone was sympathetic to my plight—we all had kids.

The years passed with many ups and downs. As I predicted, Bert worked long hours getting his struggling plastics plant on its feet. We had two more children in the following years: Judy born in 1952 and Elizabeth born in 1955. Most of our friends in those days had three or four children although a few settled for two. I became active in the community: the PTA, LWV, Citizens League, Scouts, and other community organizations. I ended up as president of a number of these organizations. Bert, too, became involved in the Cub Scouts, then Boy Scouts, when our sons were of Scout age. He even went to Boy Scout camp with their troop, Troop 6 of Pawtucket, although he would not take time off to vacation with me. He knew I understood how seriously he took his obligations. That annoyed me, but I was glad that at least he was with our boys.

Bert attended Camp Yawgoo as a boy. It was the only camp his family could afford, and it had been the highlight of Bert's summer—a wonderful experience. It was a no-frills camp that every boy could enjoy. In 1948 he became active in Camp Jori, a camp for the Jewish Orphanage of Rhode Island. It became a community camp when the orphanage closed in the late thirties. His involvement in the camp lasted sixty years.

I happily stayed at home until my youngest went into the first grade and was gone in school all day. Suddenly, I had time on my hands. I still went to PTA meetings, but the meetings became repetitive over the years. At one PTA meeting I looked across the room at a friend, and we started to giggle silently. We both realized that every report we heard that night, one or both of us had given over the years. I had already been president of our chapter for a couple of terms, and I no longer felt challenged by my community work.

That night, I said to Bert, "What am I going to do in the years ahead? I can't keep going to PTA meetings!"

He took me seriously and said, "Let's talk about it after the children are in bed." Later he said to me, "What do you want to do?"

I replied, "I don't know. All I have done for the past fifteen years is take care of kids. Maybe I should go into teaching."

After tossing it back and forth, I realized I had taken no education courses and only one psychology course in college. For teaching, I would have to start from scratch.

Finally Bert said, "You know you were always good in chemistry, and you have a BS in chemistry. They are going to need people in the labs at the new Brown Medical program. Why don't you go back to school and brush up on your chemistry?"

I said I would think about it, and we went to bed.

About that time, two more things happened that gave impetus to thinking about changing from a full-time, at-home mom to the possibility of a career—or at least a part-time job. Betty Friedan had just written a book, *The Feminine Mystique*. In this book the author proposed that women could have a job or career outside of the home and not be a bad wife or mother. *Aha*! I thought. *Maybe I could get a part-time job and still be home when the children returned from school.* In addition, as president of the Rhode Island Chapter of the Brandeis Women's Association, I attended a national conference on campus. At that time Brandeis, which opened its doors in 1948, did not have any alumni to speak of, so I was asked to join and enjoyed the intellectual challenge. At the conference, lectures were given by different Brandeis professors, and I chose one on recent advances in biochemistry. The field of chemistry had changed more in the previous twenty years than it had in the hundred years before that. These advances were so exciting that I remember sitting there thinking how I wished I could be part of this wonderful new scientific world.

Six months later I finally got up my courage to go see the head of the chemistry department at Brown University, Dr. Joseph Bunnett. He saw me as a guinea pig, to see if someone could come back to school almost eighteen years after getting their bachelor of science in chemistry and succeed in a rapidly advancing field like chemistry. He encouraged me to audit an undergraduate course and see how I did. I took up his challenge and at first audited a physical chemistry course; however, I took all the exams. Why that did not discourage me I will never know. My grades were not my best so far, but I did well enough that I would have passed with a B and so started my slide into the PhD program.

CHAPTER 3

Back to School

~

After the meeting with Dr. Bunnett, I illegally started back to school in the fall of 1961. I had not gone through the normal channels for admission to graduate school. Dr. Bunnett encouraged me to forge ahead and take some classes. Still being his experiment, he was pleased so far. He did not tell either the chemistry faculty or the graduate school that I was in the graduate program. In fact, not until I passed my cumulative PhD exams, the cums, did he notify them of my status.

Although I did not go through the regular admission channels, I paid for the courses and took an organic chemistry course and the last analytical chemistry course Brown offered. I was so excited about the new heady stuff in chemistry. But I had a problem—it was so exciting I wanted to learn everything! To pass the exams I needed to pick the most important concepts out of a mass of material. After some tutoring from a graduate student, I finally relearned techniques to organize the material and strategies to take exams. The following year I took the cumulative exams required of all students and passed the required number of exams to work for a PhD in chemistry.

Apparently a viable candidate for a PhD degree, the chemistry department offered me a fellowship as a teaching assistant that covered my tuition along with a small stipend. The third year, they awarded me a Union Carbide Research Fellowship. Then, I applied to and received a very prestigious and lucrative NIH Fellowship. These fellowships helped me pay college tuition for both of our sons while I was in graduate school! I had the uneasy feeling that I received the NIH Fellowship because they never received an application from a middle-aged mother for this particular grant before and did not know what to do with me. I always felt other applicants may have been more qualified. I did not fit into any of their categories. I was not male or young. It was very rare for a fellowship to go to someone who was older—let alone female.

In universities, every department structures the cums differently. By 1964, the year I started taking my exams, the chemistry department just changed from a schedule of taking a monthly exam for two academic years to taking them for only one academic year. A professor in the sub-specialty wrote the cums, thus I took the organic exams. If I did not pass at least four of the eight exams, I would have had to finish my research, received a master's degree, and then shown the door. If I passed the required number, I would continue my research in earnest, and after I made suitable progress (no research is ever truly finished), I would write my thesis and defend it before the chemistry faculty. Then at the next graduation, I would acquire the fancy piece of paper that proclaimed to the world in Latin that I now had the coveted doctor of philosophy in chemistry.

I'd be lying to say this process was not stressful. Many times during the process, I said to Bert, "I can't do it. I really can't do it."

He would calmly say, "Of course you can. Just take the time you need, and I'll take over for a while."

I struggled through, and in late May 1968 I walked across the outdoor stage on the Brown quadrangle. I walked alongside Bob Hope, the movie star, and John Chafee, the governor of Rhode Island, both of whom received honorary doctorates from Brown that year. I became Phyllis R. Brown, PhD.

John Chafee, who was a classmate for one year in junior high school, said to me, "You earned your doctorate the hard way."

I replied, "No, you did! Politics is a much harder field than chemistry!"

All those years ago, when I discussed with Bert what my future might hold, I did not plan or even dream of getting a PhD. It never occurred to me to tackle the pursuit of such an advanced degree. I eased into it serendipitously, one tiny step at a time.

At the first meeting with Joe Bunnett, I initially said to him that I wanted to brush-up on my chemistry, but added, "I can never go back to school full-time." Years later when we got together at meetings or conferences, he would tease me about that statement. He would say, "Whatever happened to 'I can never go back to school full-time?'"

Dr. Bunnett guided me on my choice of courses and mentored me the first couple of years. When I had to choose a research professor, I asked him if I could join his group, and he accepted me. I liked working with his group, and for the most part, we worked well as a team. He was a physical organic chemist and gave me the project to synthesize a compound that he could use later in other experiments. Although I started out with liters of solution containing the reactants, I didn't end up with the nice crystalline material I wanted but only a tarry mess.

Not long after my synthesis fizzled, Dr. Bunnett had a group meeting and announced that he was offered a position at the University of California at Santa Cruz. This opportunity was too good for him to refuse, and he would relocate in the fall. He asked each of us to come with him and finish up. Then we would receive either a degree from Brown or a degree from the University of California at Santa Cruz. Some of the group decided to go with him; however, for me it wasn't possible. Bert's business was here in Rhode Island. We could not just up and move to California, and Bert certainly did not want me to go—with or without our four children for the two years it would take me to finish up. Therefore, I had to find a new advisor in the chemistry faculty at Brown. Adamantly, I did not want to do research on polymers, enzymes, or sulfur compounds since most of them had a vile odor. There were no techniques to study polymers and enzymes yet. In those days, biochemistry was the Cinderella—the unwanted step-child—of the chemical sciences.

However, after talking to all the organic chemistry professors, I decided to work for Dr. John Edwards, a professor whose specialty was inorganic chemistry. He did not have a specific project for me, but I liked him and knew I could work well under his direction. I ended up an organic chemist working for an inorganic professor on an investigation of the reactions of a coenzyme that contained two sulfur atoms. Why did such minute amounts of that coenzyme generate such a change? Who would have believed it? My thesis, "The Investigation of Some Reactions of Alpha-Lipoic Acid," involved the formation of polymers of alpha-lipoic acid (ALA) under certain conditions. Everything I had sworn to myself to avoid! The research started me using chromatography, a technique used to separate the components in a mixture, which led me to become an analytical chemist and discover what would become the focus of my work as a chemist.

In the spring of 1967, John announced he was taking a sabbatical in Italy for the upcoming academic year and a post-doctoral fellow from Purdue would lead his group in his absence. That was not happy news for me. Since I was writing up my research at this time, my advisor and I would have heavy heated "discussions" about my thesis. The post-doc was a spectroscopist and did not understand my research. Spectroscopy is devoted to discovering the chemical composition of materials by looking at the light and other types of electromagnetic radiation they emit. Each professor had his or her own sub-specialty and was not well-versed in other sub-specialties.

After many attempts of working with the post-doc on my thesis, I had no other choice but to send it to John in Italy. This was decades before email and fax existed, and telephone calls to Italy were expensive and difficult. The mail to Italy was slow and unreliable. It sometimes took several weeks for my manuscript to reach its destination.

Seeing my frustration in trying to get corrections to my thesis back and forth across the Atlantic, Bert finally said to me, "Why don't you go to Rome and work with John on your thesis?"

I had never traveled alone, much less abroad, but I finally took the bull by the horns and arranged to go. In addition to paying my tuition and incidentals with the NIH Fellowship, I was able to fund my trip to Rome.

I think I would have quickly changed my mind if Bert or one of the girls (our boys were at college) had just once said to me, "Do you have to go?" or simply said, "Stay home." Nevertheless, they waved me goodbye, and off I went for my seven-day working adventure. John and I worked hard and by the end of the week, my thesis was in good shape. It was a week well spent and we even had a little time to go sightseeing. John, his wife Ruth, and their family treated me very well, and I gained confidence that I could handle passports, foreign money, and strange lands.

After having John accept my thesis, the next hurdle was an oral presentation to defend it. I was quite nervous. I practiced the opening sentences of my defense so often that to this day my daughter Judy can still recite them. After I successfully defended my thesis, the whole neighborhood celebrated. At graduation I received a lovely bouquet of flowers from "The Boss" and learned that it was a tradition in the chemistry department that when a woman received her PhD, her advisor sent her flowers.

The week before graduation my father, who never approved of me going back to school, said, "I'm glad you are finally graduating." When I asked why, he replied, "Well, now you can stay home."

Stunned, I inquired, "Why should I stay home?"

"Your children need you," my father said emphatically.

"But my boys are away in college, and my girls are in high school! All of them are very busy with their own lives," I said with a grin.

"But your husband needs you!" he shot back.

"Bert works long hours and doesn't need me." Then the truth came out.

"But how does it look in the community? Your husband can support you."

I was instantly amused at his Victorian attitude—the assumption that a woman would not work unless it was financially necessary!

On the other hand, my mother quietly cheered me on and was thrilled that her daughter had earned an advanced degree. Despite being ill, she insisted on going to graduation and to the party Bert threw for me that night.

When John came back from Rome, I said to him, "What am I going to do with this fancy piece of paper?" There did not seem to be any jobs on the horizon.

He said quietly, "You can never tell what door is going to open. Just be prepared to walk through it."

Sure enough, a few weeks later he heard about a job in the pharmacology section at Brown. They were looking for a chemist to synthesize or create some of the drugs they wanted to test. At the time I did not even know what a pharmacologist did, but I remembered John's words. I quickly learned what I needed to know and excitedly became a member of the section.

CHAPTER 4

Not Quite One of the Boys

~

I settled in as the chemist of the pharmacology section in the Brown medical program. After about a year, in which I struggled with purifying the drugs I made, the head of the section returned from a conference and called a meeting of the group. "I've seen an instrument," he said, "that might be useful to us. It is a nucleic acid analyzer. We could use it in purifying the drugs we are synthesizing and in following their metabolism. However, since it may not work, I have only leased it for three months. I don't want any white elephants in the lab." Since it was clear that no one in the group wanted to work with it, the section head turned to me and said, "Phyllis, it's yours. You have three months to see if it works. If it doesn't, it goes back."

The instrument, which was promptly nicknamed the white elephant, turned out to be a liquid chromatograph developed by Dr. Csaba Horváth and Dr. Seymour "Sandy" Lipsky at Yale University and designed specifically to separate and analyze nucleotides. The analyses of nucleotides, which are the building blocks of nucleic acids, were difficult.

But I knew enough about the theory of chromatography in general and liquid chromatography in particular, to know that it should work, and I was going to make it work before those three months were up.

Nucleic acids including deoxyribonucleic acid (DNA) and ribonucleic acid (RNA), are essential for all known living organisms. The information in DNA is stored as a code in four nucleobases: adenine (A), cytosine (C), guanine (G), and thymine (T). The sequence of these nucleobases determines the information available for building and maintaining an organism. Human DNA has about three billion bases and 99 percent of these bases are the same in all people. When a base attaches to a sugar molecule and a phosphate molecule, it is a nucleotide. Without the phosphate it is a nucleoside. DNA bases pair up with each other to form units called base pairs. DNA can make copies of itself with each strand of DNA serving as a pattern for duplicating the sequence of the bases. This is critical when cells divide because each new cell needs to have an exact copy of the DNA in the old cell.

It was important for us to be able to determine the nucleotides in body fluid samples when studying the effects of chemotherapeutic drugs on the body. We also were interested in analyzing nucleosides since we felt that modified nucleosides or their bases might be potent drugs in the treatment of cancer. For analysis, a process called liquid chromatography separation was used to isolate, separate, and purify these chemical compounds. The separations took place in a cold room, and sometimes it took a week to complete the analysis of a single sample for the four DNA bases. A UV spectrophotometer detected the collected fractions.

In liquid chromatography a liquid is the mobile phase, and in high-performance liquid chromatography (HPLC)—originally called high-pressure liquid chromatography—pressure is applied to push the liquid through a column containing a stationary phase. Using this technique considerably shortened the time required for the analysis as well as improved the separations. Subsequently, my specialty was in the application of chromatographic techniques to studies of biological compounds and their reactions.

I worked night and day with this instrument. It was cantankerous, and I was often frustrated and almost willing to quit. It was not dependable. At times it worked beautifully, but other times it didn't, and the results were irregular and not reproducible. Nevertheless, with the help of a group of young chemists at Varian Incorporated, who had originally purchased the machine we were leasing, I made it work. The instrument came with one page of directions for its use and three pages of instructions to purify the solvent. It was difficult to keep the instrument running well. There were many long distance calls to Varian's office in Walnut Creek, California, and several times their top service man, Dennis Gere, came bouncing into my lab, pockets filled with the parts I needed to make my chromatograph operative. Today, he would never make it past security in the airport with those bulging pockets of metal pieces, nuts, and bolts.

At the end of three months, I had enough data to write a paper. I handed the article to the section head. Several weeks went by and I heard nothing from him. I finally gathered the courage to see him in his office and ask about the paper. I had been afraid of his response. I was a mere underling in our department, and he was the chief. I explained that this was exciting research about an instrument that was useful—not only in nucleotide investigations, but also in biochemistry and biomedical research. I thought the results were hot, and if we did not submit the paper now, someone else would beat us to it by publishing similar research before we did.

He threw the paper across his desk and said to me, "Okay, submit it for publication, if you want to. But send it to one of your journals, and do not put my name on it."

My journals focused on chromatography results while his were pharmacology or biochemical journals.

Only several years later did I realize that he did not understand my research or the importance of it. Because of this, I was the sole author of the paper and became the authority on this subject. If his name had been on the paper, he would have been the senior author. Was I lucky!

I submitted the article to the *Journal of Chromatography*. Within a couple of weeks, it was accepted then published in less than three months, the fastest I ever had an article accepted or published. Right after publication I received a letter from Dr. Horváth, which arrived as I was leaving to attend a lecture that a colleague was giving. I was afraid to open it. Dr. Horváth had a reputation of being difficult. I wondered if there was something wrong with my results, if he was upset with my paper, or even if I had misspelled his name. I was certain he had found something with which he did not agree.

With trembling hands I finally opened the letter after the lecture. Inside was the nicest letter of congratulations on my excellent work. Dr. Horváth said the article would advance the use of HPLC in the biomedical sciences, and he ended by asking me for a reprint. Excited, I called him the next day to tell him how much his letter meant to me and thanked him for the words of encouragement. From then on we became good friends.

That was the beginning of my career as an analytical chemist—more specifically as a chromatographer. I wrote and published a number of articles and received invitations to speak at universities and conferences.

My first invitation to give a seminar came from the head of the biochemistry department at the University of Pennsylvania (Penn). He had read my article and wanted to know more about this new separations technique, HPLC. Among others, I received invitations to speak at MIT, Yale, and Brown.

My entrance on the international scientific stage started in 1970. The publication of my first articles on separation of nucleotides by HPLC caught the eye of the organizers of a pharmaceutical conference in Brussels, Belgium, and they invited me to speak. When I told the section head about the invitation, he immediately said that he would go and give the talk. I pointed out to him that he was not invited—I was. Politically, that was not very wise of me, but I knew he really did not understand the material in the article. No way would I allow him to take my rightful place. He gave that up when he told me not to use his name with this article.

When I realized the meeting fell between the two Jewish holidays in the fall, Rosh Hashanah and Yom Kippur, I said to Bert, "I can't go because I'm expecting the family for dinner both for Rosh Hashanah and to break the fast on Yom Kippur." He retorted, "Of course you can go. You can't pass up this opportunity." Always supportive, Bert wanted me to progress in my career. We had twenty guests for Rosh Hashanah dinner then I reset the table for the next holiday, packed my bag, and was on the plane for Brussels the next day.

Outside of my trip to Rome to finish my thesis, I had never traveled alone and especially not to Europe. A strange new world opened up for me. I knew no one at the conference. I was alone for dinners and in the evenings. It didn't bother me to be alone. Though I missed Bert's company, I knew he was taking charge at home, and that gave me great comfort.

There I met Jim Waters, founder of Waters Associates. He and his wife, Faye, lived in Massachusetts, only about seventy-five miles from me. It's amazing that I had to go all the way to Brussels to meet Jim, the CEO of the largest manufacturer of HPLC instruments and one of the most influential people in the chromatography field. From that meeting we became friends, and years later my research program started with the support of Waters Associates after accepting a position at URI as an interim assistant professor.

The talk went well, and I received very positive feedback. I successfully gave my first presentation at an international meeting. On our afternoon off I proudly went to Bruges, Belgium, alone on the train. Amazingly, that experience helped me grow and gain confidence in my professional status and in myself as a scientist.

I flew home immediately after the conference and walked through the door after a ten-hour flight just in time to take the food out of the freezer, go to services with the family, and then host about twenty people for dinner. All in a day's work!

In 1971 I hurt my back and was laid up for several weeks. Besieged with questions from all over the country on how to operate this new-fangled HPLC instrument, I decided to use this time to write a short,

easy-to-read book on HPLC; in other words, an HPLC primer. After
I put together a table of contents and wrote the first chapter, I sent my
proposal to six scientific publishers. I really had a lot of nerve—a rela-
tive unknown in the field proposing to write a book. Even though I had
lectured overseas that one time, I had just begun my journey. Five of
the publishers rejected my proposal, but the sixth, Academic Press, took
a chance on me and sent me a contract.

It took me about six months of hard work to write the first draft.
I dictated into a machine every morning for three hours before I went
to work. Then I gave the dictation to a secretary I had hired. After
she typed it up, I edited it and she retyped the corrected copy. I had
illustrations made and after that assembled it into a manuscript. Then
I sent it to six friends in the field for their feedback. Next, I incorporated their applicable suggestions or corrections into the text, which
was not easy because they did not always agree. Nevertheless, I was
finally satisfied with the manuscript and sent it off to the publisher.
In 1973 Academic Press published my book, *HPLC: Biochemical and
Biomedical Applications*, and later translated it into Japanese.

The year following the publication of my first papers on HPLC
was very productive. This opened the door to the acceptance of other
papers I wrote and continued to make HPLC known as an effective
and highly useful separation technique. We kept the chromatograph
going about twelve hours a day analyzing samples and studying the
mechanism of the separation. Our articles were circulated around the
world.

Shortly thereafter, I received a letter from Professor Eric Guiler
of the University of Tasmania, Department of Biochemistry, asking me
to collaborate on some research they were doing on the Tasmanian
devil. Yes, it is a real animal, not just the cartoon character on a children's television show. The devils had very high levels of an enzyme,
acid phosphatase, in their blood, and they wanted to know the effect
of this enzyme on the nucleotide levels. This interested us because the
only other time such high levels of this enzyme appeared was in human
males with prostate cancer. Since I was in the biochemical pharmacology

unit at Brown, we thought we might be able to use the devils as a model in cancer studies.

I worked with Professor Guiler and his team for several years, and in 1978 I wrote a proposal for a travel grant funded by the National Science Foundation (NSF). Bert and I took three wonderful trips to Tasmania between 1979 and 1982, and I did some interesting research on the devils. We never identified a correlation between the acid phosphatase and the nucleotide levels, but we were able to catalogue various animals on their family tree in relation to their nucleotide levels. Our work was well received in the biochemical world.

In the early 1970s I submitted abstracts (brief summaries) to two international chromatography meetings, one in Houston and one in Toronto, run by Dr. Albert Zlatkis. Both were accepted, and I presented my research at both meetings. There I met top chromatographers who did not know what to make of me. They were all white males, either physical or analytical chemists or engineers, and here I was, a middle-aged female organic chemist interested in applying their technique to biochemical problems. They were unsure if I was a credible scientist or why I was there.

After the Toronto meeting I received an invitation from Dr. J. Calvin Giddings of the University of Utah to write a review chapter on "The Use of HPLC in Pharmacology" for one of the books in a series called *Advances in Chromatography* published by Marcel Dekker. This invitation thrilled and honored me. It was the first chapter in that series written on the application of HPLC to real-life problems. Dr. Giddings, a top theoretician in chromatography and highly respected in the field, was the editor of the series. After the publication of the book, he wrote me a lovely letter regarding my contribution. We became good friends, and I later became a co-editor and, subsequently, editor of the series.

Life, however, in the pharmacology section at Brown became difficult. Discrimination reared its ugly head, and I found that success came at a price. By being so successful the section head, as well as a few others, saw me as a threat. Yet, if I had not been productive, they would label me a dilettante. I could not win.

CHAPTER 5

Life on the Tenure Track

~

Although my research at Brown went well, I stirred up a hornet's nest with the section head when I insisted on going to Brussels. It worsened as he saw other speaking invitations arrive for me. He started to criticize my research and writing—even as peer-reviewed journals accepted those very same articles. With the exception of the first few articles when he insisted I not include him as an author, now he wanted his name on everything I wrote, so I always included his name on anything I wrote. My curriculum vitae grew with articles in some of the best scientific journals; however, work became difficult for me. When a friend of mine, a social worker, heard of his behavior, she said to me, "Get out of there! He is passive-aggressive and will cause you more trouble as time goes by."

I thought she was overreacting, and I paid little attention to her advice. I did discuss my problem with another colleague who said to me, "Don't you realize that you are a threat to him? He thinks you want his job." That was the last thing I wanted. I just wanted to hold on to the job I had and have the freedom to do it well.

The working environment in the pharmacology section continued to spiral downward. On the one hand I became increasingly successful in my work as a pharmacologist and gained recognition for it on both the national and international fronts. On the other hand my boss criticized almost everything I did. I had inquired about a promotion, only for him to tell me that I did not need a promotion because my husband could support me.

In the meantime a new position in the pharmacology department opened, and the person hired would be on track for the tenure. Having tenure was one of the goals in academia because it assured security for a lifetime. My current position was a research appointment. I could be let go at any time, if grant money ran out. There was no job security. The letter that went out to the colleagues of my section head asked if they had any "braves" for his department. An additional position became available. Clearly, the letter was sexist indicating he wanted only males to apply. I felt he summarily rejected my application for the job simply because of my gender. In those days national searches and the consideration of minority candidates were not required and filling positions via the old boy network was most common.

My letter of rejection said that they appreciated my application and my good work as a scientist, but I was "not vital to the mission of the section." I was outraged since my contributions had been numerous. Shortly after this I attended the Women in Sciences and Medicine conference at the New York Academy of Sciences (NYAS), the most prestigious scientific society in the United States. Professor Phil Davis of Penn spoke on discrimination, and I was amazed when he said, "One of the things you will hear is that you are not vital to the mission of the department." My boss was not even original! Discrimination happened to me and I did not even recognize it!

About a week after I returned from New York, I stood in line at the small post office station near my lab. I overheard a group talking about discrimination at Brown and about a class action suit in the works. I inquired about it and found that the treatment I experienced was not unique. A woman in the anthropology department, as well as women in several other departments, also raised charges of discrimination. Gender discrimination was widespread throughout the university. I became involved in the lawsuit.

Although I was one of the four women who originally filed the class action suit against Brown, I was part of the group that grieved the action. After presenting my grievances to a panel of professors, they told me I had the clearest case of discrimination the panel heard, but they could not recompense me because I did not prove disclosure. I was never certain what that meant, and I could have appealed their decision; however, the verdict came right after my father's death, and I did not have the strength to fight it. Though his death was expected, the end was still a major blow to me and my family, and it took time for us to recover. The legal action had been wearing me down, and the two events so close together were overwhelming. Since the worry and involvement of the legal wrangling prevented me from being more productive in my career, I decided enough was enough and closed the book on this encounter with discrimination. Bert had been supportive from the beginning of this fight, but he knew how much it affected me and was glad to end this chapter of our lives.

In the end, the lessons I learned from this episode were invaluable. If I had not personally experienced discrimination, I never would have known how destructive it could be. Before I lived through that part of my life, I believed that if you were productive, did your homework, and knew your politics by keeping your nose clean and staying out of the line of fire, you would succeed. However, I learned firsthand how discrimination could prevent success, can destroy a career—even destroy a person. You cannot control discrimination and you rarely win.

Thinking back to before the lawsuit, many incidents in the pharmacology section should have been red flags warning me of the unhealthy environment. For example, one day my lab book was missing. I looked everywhere but could not find it. All my work from the past month was in it, and I was desperate! Fortunately, I visited the office of a colleague to discuss an experiment we recently completed, and there was my lab book, in the middle of his desk. When I asked what it was doing there, he coldly said I left it there, but I knew I hadn't been in his office since it disappeared. I immediately grabbed my book and left.

Later that day, while speaking with a department secretary, I glanced at the manuscript she was typing only to discover that it used the data from my lab book. While the book did contain some work we did jointly, he wrote *our* data, without showing it to me and without my name! He took the results I had worked days to obtain without even acknowledging me, much less making me a co-author. I was furious! I stormed back into his office and told him exactly what I thought. He was insolent, and as far as he was concerned, he was an innocent party to my sloppiness in leaving my lab book lying around.

Uncertain how to best handle it, I shared what happened with our boss. He listened to my story but was noncommittal. Before the end of the week, however, the secretary gave me the article with my name as a co-author. To add insult to injury, now my colleague also included his wife and son as co-authors. While both of them had helped with some tasks in the lab, neither one of them understood the work nor could they discuss or defend it if questioned. We never spoke of the incident again, but it made me wary of trusting anyone in the lab and of continuing to work there.

A few months later I attended another meeting at the NYAS on nucleotide metabolism. My boss, the section head, was there to present a paper on the metabolism of some purine analogs that we were testing as chemotherapeutic agents. The credited authors of his paper included all of my co-workers in our lab, but not me. I discovered with bittersweet irony that he based all of the results he presented on my research. The longer I sat there, the more hurt and angry I became. I mulled over if there was a way to let the audience know it was really my work. Just as my boss finished speaking, I raised my hand and added some pertinent information to his talk. As soon as the talk ended, a number of fellow chemists rushed over to me and said they recognized early on that he was presenting my research. My boss never acknowledged me or gave me credit for the work I had done—yet another push out the door of the pharmacology section.

In the spring of that same year, my boss and I both presented papers at a conference in Israel. Since he did not fully comprehend all of the data I had provided him in support of his paper, and we were on the same flight over, I thought we would discuss our papers. There was plenty of space and few distractions on the plane, yet he hardly acknowledged that he knew me. Dr. Gertrude Elion, who later won a Nobel Prize for her work on chemotherapeutic agents, chaired the session at which we presented our papers.

When someone asked me a question regarding my talk, my boss jumped up and started to answer. I was delighted when Dr. Elion strongly and emphatically stated, "Those questions are for Dr. Brown. Please let her answer."

I had to laugh to myself knowing that it was a good thing that she did, because he really did not understand my research. He would have muddied the waters instead of clarifying them. Our work was very well received, and I gained international recognition because of it—not only for my work on the analysis of nucleotides, nucleosides and their bases but also for my work on the biochemistry of these compounds. This research went on to show promising results in the development of chemotherapeutic drugs for the treatment of cancer.

At the meeting of a pharmacology group held in Michigan, both my boss and I were there. After my talk the head of the meeting came over to me, congratulated me on a fine paper, and asked my boss, "Why isn't Phyllis a member of the American Society of Pharmacology and Experimental Therapeutics (ASPET)?" I eagerly agreed to join the Society while my boss sat there looking glum. He appeared not happy about me breaking into another of his boys' clubs. During the following years I spoke at several ASPET meetings since my work straddled both fields.

Not long after this it became clear to me that my career path in the pharmacology department at Brown had hit a brick wall. Although I enjoyed my work and was proud to be a part of the Brown family, I could no longer quietly endure such blatant discrimination. My life became so miserable—the more success I achieved in the outside world, the more difficult it was at work. The situation became untenable, and I believed I had no choice but to find a new position.

Interestingly, about that time Dr. Lily Hornig, the wife of Brown's president, told me about an opening in the analytical division of the chemistry department at URI and recommended that I apply. Dr. Hornig was a PhD chemist who had also experienced problems as a female scientist in academia and well aware of the problems I had. I took her advice to heart and applied.

After I gave a seminar at the URI Chemistry Department and completed my interview with the members of the faculty, they offered me the position. The job was only available for one year. It filled the position left open when Dr. Douglas Rosie was promoted to assistant vice president of the university. He wanted to move into administration but also wanted the option of returning to teaching, in case he decided he preferred that to administrative work. While the offer confirmed my abilities, a part of me quietly hoped I could find a way to continue at Brown.

That same week I told the section head about my job offer, hoping he would encourage me to stay at Brown, but the next day, much to my dismay, he announced to the group I was leaving to go to URI—he could not wait to get rid of me. Thus, he made the decision for me. The salary offer at URI was much lower than I earned at Brown, but it never even occurred to me to negotiate a better salary. Being a docile female, it was not in my genes to be confrontational or demanding, and in the end I delighted in getting away from that section head.

In August 1974 I left for URI. In two short weeks I had to finish my research at Brown, move into my new lab at URI, and prepare to teach a freshman class in chemistry, along with a graduate course in separations. I took over URI's former crime lab filled with evidence of crimes from yesteryear. I could hardly make my way to my desk at the back of the lab. I had no money, no working space, no instruments, no grants, and no students. If not productive, it was clear that I would be gone at year's end. In addition, my first grandchild was due that Labor Day weekend and Elisabeth, our youngest daughter, had announced she was going back to college.

Looking back, I wonder how I ever got through that period, but somehow—with Bert's help and support, I did. He took Elisabeth to visit a couple of colleges that would accept her even that late in the summer; we joyfully greeted the arrival of our first grandchild, Emily, on September 2; and I hunkered down and finished my notes and syllabi for the two classes that I would be teaching. Having never taught either one, I started from scratch.

I never felt I was a great teacher for the freshman course. Not only had I never taught a freshman chemistry course, I had never taken one either. I had tested out of it at Simmons College many years before. However, I was fortunate when it came to my graduate course. I had six bright, hardworking students who helped me plan and run the course. As soon as I had the materials for the classes in order, I called all my friends in the chromatography instrument companies and told them of my predicament. I asked them if they would loan me an instrument to use for the year. Three responded positively: DuPont, Varian, and Waters all agreed to help. DuPont sent me an old instrument, but not long after the company got out of the instrument business, so service and parts were not available. Varian sent me their old "urine analyzer," which gave us a lot of trouble. However, when I asked Jim Little, the vice president at Waters for an instrument, his only question was, "When do you want it?" Of course I said immediately, and Waters not only sent me a brand new chromatograph but also set it up and serviced it. I did not make the connection at the time, but any articles I published that referenced their instrument meant free advertising for their product and helped their sales. Giving me an instrument was far less expensive than buying advertising in scientific journals, and being scientists, the readers trusted my research more.

Meanwhile, I set up my graduate students with projects and they did enough research that every one of them presented their results at the next meeting of the Pittsburgh Conference on Analytical Chemistry and Applied Spectroscopy (PittCon) in Cleveland in March of 1974. Because they put all our papers in one session, we made quite an impression on our session chair, and he noted that the university from the smallest state had the largest number of speakers. This was our debut on the national scene. The graduate students did such a good job, and it was such a great learning experience that for each PittCon meeting until I retired, I had my students submit papers and present those accepted. Every year we also submitted papers or posters at all the HPLC meetings held in the United States. It was wonderful and valuable training for my students.

Preparing for these presentations became part of the curriculum in my graduate courses. I always told my students that it was not enough to do good science; they had to write it up as a paper or as an abstract for a presentation. This is how you communicate with other scientists and show the scientific community the results of your research. I told them others would question our work, and they had to learn not only how to present their work but also how to defend it. There are times they might have to admit that they needed to do more research or that their conclusions were not valid, but the most important thing my students had to learn was not to take criticism personally—it was their science being criticized not them. I found that this lesson was not only true in science, but also a good life lesson for my students and myself.

Surprisingly, I observed that the women in my class were more apt to personalize criticism. The men did not seem to internalize the criticism; it usually appeared to roll right off their backs. I worked hard to build up the self-esteem of the women who often thought they were at fault that their paper was criticized—or worse, not accepted. We always rehearsed our presentations in front of the class, and I found the other students were more critical of their peers' work than the outside scientists. I taught critical thought so it was fresh in their mind, but these students were also more familiar with the material presented than the average scientist. After one of my students gave his talk to the class, another student raised his hand and said, "That was an excellent talk, well put together, but I didn't understand at all what you did." I guess I had given them a thorough understanding on how to give a well-structured talk, but his science was not rock solid. It was back to the drawing board for that talk.

I always instructed students not to write out their talk and then read it, just have cues on note cards or slides. However, one young man typed out his entire talk and then started to read it word-for-word while on stage. When he looked up at the screen, he lost his place in the talk. He started to sweat, and it looked as if he would faint. First, he loosened his tie and then unbuttoned the top buttons of his shirt. Finally, the poor student seemed paralyzed, and the chair kindly inquired if he would like a moment to get a cold drink. When the student did not return after ten minutes, the chairman asked if I would like to finish the talk.

Breaking the tension of this moment, I said, "I always wondered what second authors were for. Now I know." Everyone laughed and luckily, I knew the material well enough to pick up where he left off and finish the talk. No student of mine ever read a paper again.

About five years later I received a call from a student who had received her PhD while studying under me. I wondered what she wanted—a reference for a new job, perhaps? Finally, she said, "Dr. Brown, I wanted to call and thank you. I just interviewed a chemist for a job in my department. His seminar was so awful that I thought: *'If he had been Dr. Brown's student, he never would have given such a bad seminar.'* I didn't realize everything that you were trying to teach us when I took your classes, but I certainly do now." That was quite a confession because she had indeed been difficult, resistant, and resentful when she was in class. Her comment made all my years of teaching worthwhile.

In addition to teaching my freshman and graduate course, we had to set up my laboratory, which meant cleaning out all the crime lab equipment. A couple of professors from the Pharmacy School offered to help me, and another provided me with some initial supplies, as I had no money to start my research. Today, new faculty in the chemistry department receive sizeable grants to buy equipment, supplies, and remodel their laboratories. I received nothing. Whether that was because they did not expect me to stay, or they just did not do it in those days, I do not know. Regardless, I succeeded by begging and borrowing whatever I needed and by running my research on a shoestring budget. The ability for me to do any research was entirely a miracle. In every spare moment I wrote grant proposals. Although at Brown trained personnel would help you write proposals and apply for grants, at URI there were none. On my own, I sent out proposals far and wide to big and small foundations and agencies. I was totally naïve on the politics of funding and stunned when a small foundation in New Haven rejected my grant proposal, but the Yale professors who reviewed my proposal stole the research I proposed. I innocently believed in the honesty of all scientists and stealing an idea from a research proposal never occurred to me. Did I have a lot to learn. Science can be a cutthroat endeavor, and you must guard your flanks.

I sent a good-sized grant proposal to the NIH for work I started at Brown. Much to my surprise, the NIH awarded me the funds, and the only negative comment was their surprise that my budget was so small. They did not understand how I would accomplish all I proposed on such a low funding amount. I thought I asked for a large amount of money, but the NIH increased the amount they were giving me! I later learned that at that time, it was the largest NIH grant ever funded at URI. The grant covered three years, and the NIH renewed it for another three years.

Before the end of my first year, the boys in the URI administration offered to renew my contract and put me on the tenure track. They could do things like that in the early 1970s. Now they have to advertise the job and do a national search. Back then, that was not necessary. I later found out they renewed my contract the first year because the university did not want to lose the analytical position in the chemistry department, as well as all the instruments I had somehow borrowed. If I went elsewhere, the instruments would have gone with me. In addition, I began to receive grants and those research funds added to my allure.

I was delighted to accept URI's offer since I was just beginning to settle in. Most of the chemistry faculty were very nice to me, especially the head of the department and chair of the search committee, both of whom recommended I be hired. However, a few of the men—and there were only men on the staff then—never acknowledged my presence until I became a permanent staff member. In retrospect, I was much too busy to notice even if someone did snub me. I also was not aware that I received a much lower salary than men who had nowhere near my qualifications. By the time I started at URI, I had published my first book, written more than twenty articles, been awarded numerous research grants, and had spoken at conferences all over the world. Sadly, I never did catch up to the men's salary while at URI, even though I was more qualified than a number of the male chemists. At the time I was too naïve to inquire about it and fight for a better salary and benefits. Within three years I was promoted to associate professor with tenure, and after another three years promoted to full professor. Although within the first few years I received the URI prize for research, as well as national and international awards, my salary never matched my male colleagues. It was not until I retired that I found out exactly how much less I had made over the years than my comparable colleagues.

Because of my first graduate class, the success of my students at PittCon, and because I had written a book, I began to attract graduate students. Those first students really took a chance working for a new professor with no tenure. How did they know I would still be at URI in the later years of their research? Nevertheless, I took over Doug's students, Bob and Ante, and then new graduate students Rick and Joy joined my group. When my first grant was funded, a technician and a post-doc were added to my group, and I was off and running!

My lab became the hub of the analytical division of the chemistry department at URI. It buzzed with activity and excitement. I never worked so hard in my life—writing grants, teaching both undergraduate and graduate courses, guiding my graduate students—and I was never happier. I loved every aspect of my job and worked long hours. It became apparent to Bert that living in Pawtucket was impossible if I was to succeed, so he found an apartment for us in Narragansett. It did not take long for us to realize that our neighbors were difficult, to say the least. They fought every night, yelling at each other, slamming doors, and taking off in the car with tires screeching. Bert decided we needed our own home and started looking for land to build a house.

He found a scenic lot in Narragansett on the road to Camp Varnum, a Rhode Island National Guard facility, and we had a Deck House built, which was a pre-fabricated home.

It was a lovely house, set on a little rise among two acres of land. However, Bert was not satisfied with development of the surrounding land and when he saw a beautiful lot high up overlooking the West Passage of Narragansett Bay, we bought it. I was quite upset; we had just moved into the newly built home, and here he was thinking of moving again. Unexpectedly, we had an excellent offer to buy our house, and they wanted it completely furnished—dishes, linens, furniture, and even Bert's tractor, which he loved. As it happened, Bert and I lived in San Diego the next year while I was on sabbatical, so we had fun planning the new house. When we came back to Narragansett in the fall of 1980, construction started on our dream house. It was also a Deck House but quite different in design from the first. It was completed in early summer 1981, and we lived there for twenty glorious years.

CHAPTER 6

Have Slides, Will Travel

~

In the early 1970s, I went to an Eastern Analytical Symposium (EAS) in Atlantic City. As an invited speaker I attended a VIP cocktail party at the end of the first day. The chromatographers present clustered in one corner away from the other analytical chemists, and as the party ended they decided to go out to dinner. Since I was the new kid on the block and a middle-aged woman to boot, they did not know what to do with me. These chromatographers had been working together for several years and knew each other well—not to mention they were all men. They were instrumentalists or theorists, but there were no application specialists in the group—until I came along.

When we prepared to leave, one of them clumsily said, "You don't want to go out to dinner with us, do you?"

I replied that of course I wanted to go but told him I would pay my own way. I felt a collective sigh of relief because they did not know how to handle paying for me. None of them wanted to dip into their expense accounts to pay for me, yet each seemed to be wondering if, being a woman, I expected someone to pay for me, as was done in those years. Rarely did a woman go Dutch.

We went to a very nice Italian restaurant. One wall displayed an inviting pastoral scene, and the opposite wall featured a bevy of luscious, beautiful nude ladies. My colleagues quickly maneuvered me to face the pastoral scene. Once we all were seated and had ordered drinks, I asked, "Did you seat me facing the pastoral scene because you were worried the nude scene would offend me or because you didn't want to waste the lovely ladies on me?" They all cracked up, and it broke the tension of having me—a woman—in their good ol' boys' club.

When I called home later that night, I said, "Bert, I am now one of the boys," and recounted what had happened.

That night marked the beginning of my acceptance into the rarefied, upper echelon of the chromatography inner circle, and I made some very good friends. From then on I was included in most of their private get-togethers at professional meetings large and small. Up until then, if I had been at a conference without Bert, I would usually eat dinner alone. There were no other women to befriend, and the men went off by themselves. I did not realize until later that I had missed important discussions about what was going on in the chromatography world—new developments in instrumentation and new advances in the field. I especially missed out on the planning of upcoming conferences— the theme of the meeting, the keynote speakers, possible chairs for each session, etc. There was also gossip that could be helpful to a career. Most importantly, I could make connections with the players in the field.

I am not sure how I had the nerve to speak at national and international meetings. Luckily, I'm not the nervous type, so speaking at these meetings was more of a challenge; it was like taking a test and seeing if my research stood up to the scrutiny. It was quite an accomplishment when it did. At URI no one fully understood my research, so I did not have anyone who could critically understand what I did. Until I presented my findings, I was unsure of how it would be received that is, until my participation in these chromatography meetings started in the early 1970s.

I went to the Brussels symposium to present my original research on the separation of nucleotides by HPLC. I did not know a soul in the audience, yet my paper was very well received. There I saw a notice about an upcoming chromatography conference in Toronto. I was still doing research at Brown—for an assistant professor to gain recognition was a rare occurrence. Papers on any phase of chromatography were invited, and I rashly sent in an abstract on the work I had done on the separation of nucleotides. Much to my surprise, it was accepted. I was a newbie and had gained little exposure.

When I arrived at the conference, I recognized all the names of the scientists giving papers as the top people in the field whose papers I had read. *What am I doing here?* I wondered. This was a huge step into the top group of my peers. I took a deep breath, gave my paper, and answered whatever questions they asked. I was in my element. The acceptance gave me the courage I needed to continue. That night, I sat in the bar with leaders in our field that I never thought I'd meet: Nobel Prize winner A.J.P. Martin; top theorist Cal Giddings, HPLC particle pioneer Jack Kirkland, and Lloyd Snyder, author of many papers on instrumentation. Roy Keller, one of the editors of the *Advances in Chromatography* book series, and Victor Pretorius, leading chromatographer from Pretoria, South Africa, were there too.

I could not believe I was with such prominent scientists. What a thrill for a novice like me! I did not know it then, but I was doing what is called networking in today's world. I later learned that this interaction with my colleagues was the most important part of any conference. Bert shared my joy by phone each day I was away. This meeting started me on the pathway to the exciting participation in international science. After that I knew I wanted to be in the international science field, and when chances came to take the administrative path, I always turned it down to keep my focus on the science.

The next meeting was in Houston because the organizer of this particular series of meetings, Dr. Zlatkis, was on faculty at the University of Houston. I clearly remember that my presentation was the last one on the last day, the most unwanted spot in a program because the audience dwindles toward the end of a symposium. The curious had remained in their seats; they wanted to see what I had to offer. I learned to make certain the title of my talk was intriguing. They'd had enough chatter. The chromatograms I showed were different from all the others shown. They were not pretty. I called them lumpy and humpy, whereas the others were sharp and clean. Mine were real compounds in real samples, and the others had used clean samples. I also opened with the statement, "I always wondered who has the last speaking spot on a program. I have now found out. It is the one who gives the most different talk, hoping some attendees would be curious enough about this talk so there would be an audience."

My speaking career took off in the early 70s, when I received an invitation to speak at a small meeting arranged by Varian held at of all places the Playboy Club in New Jersey. There we were—all these male scientists, the Bunnies, and me. It was my only visit to one of Hugh Hefner's Playboy Clubs. I was probably the only person fully focused on the presentation.

In the days before PowerPoint, you used slides to illustrate lectures and talks. My mottos for the years between 1973 and 2001 were *Have slides, will travel*, and *See the world through chemistry and chromatography*. The last thing I expected when I went to URI was to travel as much as I did. I was so naïve when I started, but I learned quickly. My friend Jim Fasching, professor emeritus at URI, taught me the ropes about presenting my research at PittCon and especially about taking my graduate students there. We did not have much money for travel, but we scrimped and begged for funding from any source. I am still not sure how we did it.

PittCon, the largest yearly conference on analytical chemistry, started in Pittsburgh, thus the name. After a number of years, it outgrew the facilities in Pittsburgh and moved to Cleveland. Over the years the conference was held in various cities. At its height it attracted thousands of participants. Manufacturers first exhibited the latest developments in instruments here. My students managed to get all kinds of useful samples for our lab and make friends with many of the manufacturers' representatives. They always came home with exciting new ideas about research. They learned how to network and to meet the leaders in the chromatography field. Because of the students' networking and friendships, they kept our lab afloat when funding decreased or they wanted to try special parts or equipment—especially if they heard about an experimental and/or expensive column that might be useful. An HPLC column was a metal tube that held the stationary phase—the area where the separations of the compounds took place.

Because of the contacts they made at PittCon, most of my students had no trouble landing jobs after graduation. If PittCon was within driving distance, they would pile in a car and off they went. I would generally meet up with my students at the convention. I did not travel with my students. I was not interested in knowing what they did with their personal lives. It was a wonderful learning opportunity and a great morale booster that my students eagerly looked forward to each year. After a couple of years, I was recognized and invited to speak or organize sessions at the conference. I was very excited the first time I received a personal invitation to a VIP reception, which was the Sunday evening before the conference started. I carefully chose what I was going to wear. Alas, my suitcase went to Los Angeles instead of getting off the plane with me in Cleveland, and I had to go to the reception in my travel clothes. Another time, I bought a new dress to wear when giving my presentation. Luckily, I wore it at home first. It had a front zipper, a new plastic one, which separated completely when I sat down. If I had worn it to the meeting first, I would have sat down awaiting my talk and when I went to speak, the audience would have seen me in my panties and Maidenform bra!

The PittCon meetings were fun, educational, and exciting. Session chairs wanted to include my students in their sessions because they knew that the students were always well prepared and professional. These sessions were the place to give presentations and learn about new developments in the field.

In 1976, after I had been at URI three years, I received a letter from the Royal Australian Chemical Society inviting me to give the plenary lecture at their annual Analytical Chemistry Meeting. I was thrilled with this honor. In my heart, I knew I was a good speaker and could present new material in an interesting way. I called Doug Rosie, now permanently a vice president of URI and said, "Doug, I just received this invitation to speak in, of all places, Sydney, Australia."

He promptly said, "You're going, aren't you?"

I retorted, "How can I go? I am teaching a large freshman class."

To which he replied, "I'll teach it for you. I taught that course for years and can do it easily. You owe it to URI to represent them at this meeting."

After I hung up I reread the letter and found they even offered me free business class airfare and all expenses paid for ten days in Australia. When I told Bert about the invitation, he was delighted and said, "Of course we will go." That was the beginning of our Australian adventures. These trips were relatively inexpensive, with Bert's airfare being our only expense. Bert thoroughly enjoyed the trips offered for the spouses while the meetings were going on. It did not hurt that there were mainly women on these trips. Bert loved my success and proudly proclaimed it to the world whenever he had a chance.

When the organizers announced that I was going to be speaking in Australia, I also received invites to speak at universities in Adelaide, Melbourne, and Canberra. Since Bert sold his business and was now semi-retired, we decided to make a vacation out of the trip and added New Zealand and Fiji to our itinerary.

Just before we left I applied for and received our first American Express (Amex) credit card. Bert and I already had both Visa and MasterCard, but I did not know whether they were as widely accepted globally as the Amex card. We were lucky I had one because many places only accepted Amex. When we returned home after being gone six weeks, our telephone answering machine overflowed with calls from Amex. All of a sudden on a brand new credit card, there were all these charges in Australia, New Zealand, and Fiji. The company was concerned that someone had stolen our card and was having quite a fling with it. We reassured them that we were responsible and would pay the bill. This experience taught me to call Amex to let them know if we were going away for an extended length of time. We were fortunate that they did not freeze our credit when we were so far away.

Once Bert and I got over the jet lag from the over twenty-hour flight, we had a glorious time. The Australian scientists were most hospitable; they wined and dined us and showed us the sights. Bert looked up some former business friends and one of them tried to persuade us to buy a condominium in Brisbane on Australia's Gold Coast. It probably was a good buy but not for us!

I had enthusiastic audiences wherever I spoke, except at the National University in Canberra. After my talk, my host, whom I had known in the United States when he was a post doc in the chemistry department at Brown, said snidely, "Nice technique but we don't need it for our work."

I remember thinking to myself: *Brother, you really need this technique. Your research would reach new levels.* Nevertheless, his inflexibility prevented him from trying it. He thought he knew better than I did; whether it was personal or a female thing, I was never sure. A couple of years later, however, I received a request from him for more information on HPLC. He thought they "might give it a try." I laughed thinking how much time he had lost.

New Zealand and Fiji were purely vacation, and the sights were marvelous. On our flight from Fiji, however, we heard a loud noise and saw a flash of fire. Bert immediately saw the seriousness of the situation and said to me quietly, "I think we have lost an engine. Not long afterwards, the pilot announced on the radio that we had indeed lost one engine, and we limped back to Fiji. Luckily, we were able to get on another flight but to San Francisco instead of Los Angeles. The majority of the passengers had to wait for another flight because the repairs to that plane could take a week or more.

The Australian saga continued when my friends in Tasmania later asked me to write a joint travel grant to submit to the National Science Fund (NSF). During the Great Blizzard of 1978, Bert and I were snowed in at home, and fortunately, I had all the information with me that I needed to write the proposal. A few weeks later I sent it in and promptly forgot about it. The following August I was in Jerusalem and through friends met a man who worked at NSF. When he heard my name, he asked, "Are you the Tasmanian devil lady?"

I laughed and said, "I guess so."

He asked me why I had not responded to a message left for me when he called to tell me that they had approved my grant. I had been out of the country and never received that message. The grant gave us money for three trips to Tasmania, as well as trips to URI for the Tasmanians. He also asked me if I noticed anything different about the proposal. Since I did not, he said the NSF staff thought the title "Investigation of the Nucleotide Metabolism of the Tasmanian Devil" would earn a Golden Fleece Award, an award meant to ridicule what then-Senator William Proxmire deemed as a wasteful use of taxpayer money. I cannot remember the new title, but it was quite innocuous. Although we did not get the expected results from our joint research, it was productive in other ways and resulted in several published articles in prestigious journals. On the second trip to Australia, Bert and I visited Tahiti on our way home. On the third trip we went to Australia via Europe, where I attended a meeting in Barcelona and visited Perth before flying across the Australian continent.

When we were in Tasmania, Dr. Guiler's associate in this research project, Dr. John Sallis, adopted us. John, along with his family, were our hosts and tour guides. I worked closely with him for many years. Since we became good friends, we were delighted to host them and showed them the beauty of Rhode Island when they came to visit as part of the research project.

The Australian experience was the beginning of our international travel where we made many friends. There were two other meetings that I attended regularly: those of the American Chemical Society (ACS), which met twice a year, and the HPLC meetings that convened every spring. I only went to the ACS meetings when there were interesting sessions on HPLC, or a colleague I knew won an award. For about ten years straight, one of the top chromatographers in the field submitted my name for the ACS chromatography and separations awards. Nevertheless, I was always a bridesmaid and never the bride, in that I was always a finalist, but never recognized officially by my professional society for my work. It has only been over the last five to ten years, that that venerable body has recognized women for their achievements in chemistry. In fact, when I was appointed to the board of the prestigious journal *Analytical Chemistry*, I looked up its history and found that in the many years of its existence, only four women had served on this board. When I mentioned that fact to another member of the board, he laughed and said, "Knowing the people involved, I am surprised there were that many!"

Finally, there is a little more female representation. Even now when I get a journal with a program listing the awards for the year, I always look to see how many women are on the board of that journal, how many women are speaking at the meeting, how many chairing sessions, and how many received awards. The numbers were amazingly small until the last few years when progress in this area became evident. I became aware of this problem in the mid-1970s, and about forty years later, we finally begin to see the results of our efforts to break the glass ceiling.

I tried not to miss the yearly HPLC meetings, which are held alternately in Europe and the United States. These meetings were small, and a core group of the top chromatographers organized, ran, and attended them. The members vied with each other to organize and chair the meetings, which they planned several years in advance. In addition, chromatographers competed to hold the most original and extravagant opening ceremonies, general receptions, and dinners for the VIP members. This gathering, called simply HPLC followed by the year in which it was held, started as a general chromatography meeting organized and chaired by Dr. Al Zlatkis of the University of Houston. At first, he did everything for the meeting—planned it, invited the speakers, arranged for the meeting place, etc. In the early 1980s when the interest in HPLC began to grow, a small group of chromatographers broke off and started meetings limited to HPLC. The meetings were small, exclusive, and by invitation only. In fact, I did not even know about the meetings until a friend, a manufacturer's representative, told me about them.

At another meeting I overheard a couple of the top chromatographers talking about the HPLC meeting coming up. I stopped and "innocently" asked about the HPLC meeting and one of them said, "Would you like to go?" Of course I said yes, and they invited me to the next meeting in New Jersey. Of all things, the wedding of our youngest daughter, Elizabeth, was the weekend following the meeting. Hers was a large affair held at our home. As the mother of the bride, I had a lot to do, especially since Elizabeth was busy in graduate school. However, Bert convinced me I should go to the meeting, and off I went. Quite a debut for me at the HPLC meetings being the only woman in attendance! As usual, they treated me like one of the boys.

I knew a number of the men attending the meeting, since in previous years I had submitted abstracts to the general chromatography meetings held in Toronto and Houston. I was quite an oddity; a middle-aged woman trained as an organic chemist who used their new instruments to study biochemical and pharmacological problems. The other participants were white males with degrees in physical or analytical chemistry or engineering, and all worked on theoretical or instrumental research. I stood out like a sore thumb. These men seemed uncertain of how to treat a woman as a colleague and equal. Some of them seemed to wonder if I was even a real scientist.

The HPLC meetings were held in many interesting European locations: Edinburgh, Amsterdam, Barcelona, Cannes, Maastricht, etc. Sweden was the only one I missed in Europe.

In Edinburgh I talked with the organizer of the next meeting about inviting women to chair a few of the sessions. He agreed and invited two other women to be chairpersons. He called me before the meeting, very worried about how they would do in this position, and he went to each session to monitor their performance. Much to his surprise, the roof did not fall in and both women did a very good job. Sadly, at the meeting the following year, I was once again the only woman speaker and chairperson of a session. It was not until 1991 at the HPLC meeting in Basle that I was invited to be a plenary speaker at one of these prestigious meetings. But I had a conflict; Emily, my oldest grandchild, was graduating from high school the same day, and the whole family was gathering for that happy occasion. After much soul searching and discussion, Bert and I decided that he would fly back to Boston and represent us at the graduation, and I would stay in Switzerland and give the address. We were afraid that as the first woman to receive this opportunity, if I backed out, they would say, *Just like a woman* and never invite a woman to have a prominent part in the meeting again. A tough decision but I think the right one. I fought too hard and long for this opportunity to pass it up. Life is never simple!

For most of my career, I spent a part of my time working on women in science issues. At URI, along with a counselor who was a member of the psychology department, I organized a regular, brown bag luncheon and discussion group for women in science at the university; female faculty, staff, and graduate students were welcome. It was a place where any of these women could let their hair down, pour their hearts out, and get advice about how to handle a discrimination or harassment problem they encountered. We attracted women in engineering and oceanography, where there were very small numbers of women, as well as the other sciences and math.

I will never forget a brilliant oceanography student who came to us visibly upset. At the most recent oceanography school seminar, a male graduate student closed his talk with a very offensive and sexist joke. Everyone thought it was very funny except this student, the only female in the room. No one objected to it. When she spoke to her advisor about it, he shrugged and told her not to have such thin skin. She needed a broad shoulder to lean on and wanted advice about how to handle this problem, if it came up again. We all tossed it around and finally came up with a game plan, so she could get her point across and stop this type of behavior without being ostracized by her fellow students. I think we came close to losing her as a student, but giving her a safe place to go, we saved a very brilliant career. Months later, an oceanography professor thanked me for helping this student and told me the faculty had discussed this problem, and they were taking steps to prevent further harassment of women. They had not been aware of it at all.

This luncheon and discussion group was still going strong when I retired in 2001 although the group morphed into a more structured monthly meeting with a large number of women attending. It lost its intimacy and the ability of women students to discuss harassment problems and get solid, pragmatic advice. However, by 2001 there were other mechanisms in place at the university for solving these problems.

In 1991 I submitted an abstract to organize a session at PittCon on "Women in Chemistry: Why So Few? What can we do about it?" My abstract was accepted and I invited the speakers. When Henry Blount, a director at NSF, heard about the session, he asked me to include him on the program, and I was delighted to have him. They assigned us a small room tucked away under the stairs. I am certain that the organizers thought only a few would attend. Much to their surprise and mine, a half-hour before the start of the session the seats were full, and the crowd overflowed into the hallway. The session was the hit of that PittCon meeting and talked about by everyone. However, when I applied to have another session the following year, they denied my request. In years to follow they would occasionally offer a session on women in analytical chemistry, but none were as successful.

A few years earlier I wrote an article on this subject, which was published in a 1986 issue of *Trends in Analytical Chemistry*. Moreover, at each conference I tried my best to get to know the young women who were working in chromatography, in an effort to mentor and encourage them. At the HPLC '85 meeting in Edinburgh, I met a few young women in the ladies' room. We all started talking, but I had to leave because I was about to give a presentation. So I suggested that all of us meet for lunch, and we agreed upon a date, place, and time. Word quickly spread throughout the conference that I was meeting with some of the women, and much to my surprise when the time came, there were over twenty women there. We had a spirited discussion over lunch, and they enthusiastically requested that I plan a meeting of the women at the upcoming HPLC meeting in San Francisco. During the remainder of the conference in Edinburgh, more women came to me to say they wished they had known about the gathering and were sorry they missed it. We quickly dubbed this meeting, The Ladies Room Luncheon.

For the following year in San Francisco, the organizer, Professor Georges Guiochon, asked if I wanted to organize a luncheon with the women. I did organize a discussion group and lunch for the women attendees at the conference. The seats were jam-packed, and women stood in every available space.

A lone man came and plunked down in a chair in the middle of the room. He said that I could not discriminate against males, and he wanted to know what was going on. I thought it interesting that he would take time out of his busy schedule to find out what the concerns of women were. After the meeting we went to the dining room for lunch to find all the other participants already seated. We made quite a statement walking in; we let the other attendees know there were a growing number of successful women chromatographers even if I was still the only woman giving a paper at the meeting.

Since I thought only twenty-five to thirty women would attend, I did not have enough copies of the handouts for the more than one hundred women who attended. The interest this meeting demonstrated was thrilling. It was exciting to see so many women front and center who usually sat in the back of the room at these meetings. I enjoyed being a mentor to these bright young women. Although I had sent out invitations and questionnaires to all the women registered for the conference, only a small percentage answered me. I received a funny reply from a person with a unisex first name stating that the respondent would love to participate, but didn't know if he, being a male, was welcome.

All of the attendees wanted to discuss the problems they encountered as women chromatographers. Controlling the discussion was difficult, and we went way over the allotted time. I tried to keep the discussion as positive as possible; things women could do to get ahead. Many of the women, especially those from Europe, experienced these same problems in their workplace, as well as facing discrimination in the home. Their husbands did not mind if their wives held a job, but as the women earned promotions, the husbands objected to the women not being readily available for responsibilities at home. I was at a loss for what advice to offer about their problems at home—Bert was always supportive. Vicariously, Bert enjoyed my successes, as this was what he might have done if his career had taken a different path. I encouraged the women to write up their research and submit it for publication or at least as abstracts for talks at conferences.

The following year at the HPLC meeting in Amsterdam, I asked the organizers if we could again schedule a luncheon for the women. They were not interested. At the meeting, however, they sold silk articles with the HPLC logo on it—ties for the men and scarves for their wives, mothers, sisters, and daughters. Nothing was mentioned about women chromatographers. The women, who were furious at the organizers for not allowing a luncheon, as well as for their sexist statement with the scarves and ties, met quietly with me a few at a time. They obviously feared repercussions if they openly defied the ban on an official luncheon.

The following year in Baltimore, the chairperson of HPLC '86 gently satirized the role of women during a skit in the opening ceremony. The play, complete with costumes, was about Christopher Columbus and the discovery of America. I played the captain of the fourth ship, which was manned by all women. This ship was never recorded in history. It was nice to be noticed by the upper echelon of chromatographers. By performing in the skit, we brought to the forefront that there are women chromatographers who can be successful.

In 1979 I spoke at a meeting in Surrey, England. The organizers of this symposium planned an extra-special event for the attendees by taking us to the Magic Circle, an exclusive and long-standing society that still brings together the world's most talented illusionists. To join this prestigious organization, an existing member must recommend the magician, and they must pass rigorous tests. Members are sworn to secrecy to protect their craft. It was a wonderful evening. We divided into small groups and enjoyed refreshments while master magicians entertained us with card tricks and ended with a fabulous stage show that featured the most advanced illusionists. Invites to their shows are selective, and we felt honored to gain admittance.

After staying in London for a short time, we took the train to Edinburgh. Rick, one of my first graduate students, had an NSF Fellowship to do a post-doctoral year with my friend Professor John Knox at the Wolfson Chromatography Laboratory at the University of Edinburgh. John was one of the top theorists in chromatography, and it was quite an honor to work with him. All of us from URI were thrilled that Rick received this award, being the first such award given to a URI student. When John found out I was going to be in London, he invited me to Edinburgh to give a lecture to the chemistry department. Bert and I were delighted to have the opportunity to visit Scotland. Rick met us when we arrived and squired us around to see the sights. We saw the awesome castle where the Queen and her family vacationed in the summer, ate piping hot fish and chips wrapped in newspaper from a street vendor, and enjoyed touring the scenic Highlands.

Rick, a rugged farm boy, told us that if John asked to take us hill walking, tell him no.

"Why?" I asked.

He replied that while hill walking sounds quite innocuous, it was truly a rugged hike, which he found quite taxing and might be difficult for me. We took his advice. When John and his lovely wife, Jo, took a day off to be with us, they asked if we wanted to go hill walking or sightseeing. We quickly replied sightseeing, and off we went to enjoy the places in and around Edinburgh. We had a delightful time, and the dialogue between John and Jo was similar to that of Bert and me, only with a Scotch brogue—for example,

"Slow down! Didn't you see that stop sign?"

"We turn right here, not left!"

"Maybe we should stop and ask for directions?"

This was well before the days of the GPS. After a day of travels, they took us back to their home for tea, and John's students came to meet us.

On our trip with Rick to the Highlands, the roads were narrow, and when a bus came barreling at us, we hastily pulled to the side, right into a ditch. While deciding what to do, a car pulled up with four young men inside, all wearing red sweaters. They surveyed the situation, worked together, and had our car out of the ditch in no time. Then they hopped back into their car and were off before we could thank them. Problem solved!

The Highlands were lovely, and we stayed overnight at a quaint bed and breakfast in a nearby town before returning the next day with enough time to explore Glasgow on the drive back. While sightseeing, I asked John why he had invited me to speak. He knew more about chromatography than I would ever know. He responded by telling me that as a theorist, he admired my work in applications. He added that he wanted his students to meet a successful woman chromatographer. They had never had one as a speaker.

Bert and I returned to Edinburgh several more times over the years. The last time, John was chairperson of HPLC '85, and he asked me to give one of the lectures. Rick also gave a talk at that meeting, so I enjoyed getting together with him again. However, I was still the only woman participant in the program, so as always it was life with the boys.

There were also HPLC meetings held in Spain, one in Barcelona, and one in Granada. After attending the meeting in Barcelona, Bert and I traveled on to Israel and then to Australia, stopping in Greece and then Perth on our way to Tasmania.

While in Barcelona, a young man came to me and said, "You're a woman."

Surprised, I replied, "Yes, my name is Phyllis." I always used my full name, Phyllis R. Brown, so it was obvious that the author was female. In the old days many women scientists used only their initials so their articles were not summarily rejected.

Then he said, "I thought that your name was Phillipe."

I laughed and retorted that most people did not expect to see a middle-aged woman as a chromatographer.

Embarrassed, he quickly apologized and barely waited for my reply before he disappeared.

While it was rare to hear about women chemists, Erika Cremer, a physical chemist in Austria, actually built the first gas chromatograph in 1944. That fact was not widely known because her laboratory and almost all of her notes were destroyed in an air raid during World War II, which delayed publication of her work. Before the war Cremer had trouble finding a job but obtained a teaching and research position in early 1941 when all the men were serving in the military.

Bert and I enjoyed spending time in Granada to attend HPLC. It was unbelievably beautiful with the Alhambra in the middle of town. I almost missed the meeting. I told my travel agent to get tickets for Granada, but he made reservations for us to fly to Grenada in the Caribbean. It would have been a nice vacation but not the place I needed to be. Luckily, we caught the error in time to exchange our airline tickets for ones headed to the right place.

I learned about more than chromatography at the conferences I attended. At many meetings a number of the men arrived with their wives—or so I assumed. Wrong! Many of the women there were mistresses, and only a few men brought their wives. At another meeting some fellow chemists and I were chatting when John, a man I knew from correspondence but had never met, approached us. He was with a lovely young woman, and they clearly enjoyed one another's company. We all exchanged pleasantries when we met, but when John did not introduce his companion, I asked, "Aren't you going to introduce me to your wife?"

I was the only one there who did not already know their status. She was not his wife but a fellow chromatographer from another university. It turned out that they were very close friends from college, both were gay, and they simply enjoyed spending time together at meetings. Over the years I became good friends with many of the women who were regulars at these meetings.

CHAPTER 7

The Peripatetic Professor

~

My life on the speaking circuit was never dull. Some trips were short and all business. Other times Bert and I put together business with a little vacation time and traveled to places we might have otherwise never visited.

Our longest trips were those to Tasmania. To go halfway around the world and not see some of the exotic places en route would have been foolish. So on the way home from one trip, we explored Fiji, another Tahiti, and another Hawaii. We snorkeled along islands on the Great Barrier Reef off the coast of Australia. During one trip we stayed on Great Keppel Island and another on Heron Island, where they had a research station.

At Heron Island accommodations were like camp bunks, only these were small, only for two. We sat at assigned tables in the dining hall and met scientists and tourists from all over the world who came to see the wondrous underwater life—the beautiful coral and fish of all colors, shapes, and sizes. I did not know there were fish of all hues— red, pink, orange, blue, purple, etc.

Phyllis and Bert in the spring of 1942 at
Simmons College after they were engaged.

Many of the visitors at Heron Island were highly knowledgeable
and wanted to see certain fish or species. Others were like us, interested
but with little background. There were guided walking and snorkeling
trips where we saw the wonders of the shore and sea. One night, one
of the researchers took us on a walk around the island looking for the
nesting places of the great green turtles that came ashore after dark to
hatch their young. We never saw the turtles but learned a lot about them.

On the second day there, our neighbors in the nearest little
cottage said to us, "If you hear moaning in the night and noises sound-
ing like *oohs*, and *ahhs*, it isn't us. The noddy birds come in during the
night. They mate in nests in the bushes near us and then go back to
the water at dawn." I was glad they told us, or Bert and I would have
thought that the couple were having the most amorous nights.

We met another couple aboard the small plane that took us to
Great Keppel Island. They looked as if they were straight out of a

Phyllis with Eli Grushka (to her right) at the HPLC Meeting in Lausanne, 1979.

British colonial movie or a BBC television show. Very aristocratic, he had a head of white hair and a white handlebar moustache. She was dressed in a flowered voile dress and white gloves.

Bert whispered to me, "Don't get too friendly with them. We can get stuck with them and they look very stuffy."

However, we became friends, and they were anything but stuffy. Since he was the president of one of the largest chemical companies in Australia, he was interested in Bert and me because we were both chemists. It turned out that we were the only four guests on the island, and we had great fun together, but they could drink us under the table. Starting with afternoon cocktails, then a couple of bottles of wine with dinner, and ending with a nightcap. When we told them we were going to Fiji on our way home, they helped us plan our trip, suggesting a side trip to the Blue Lagoon. It was magical—unbelievably beautiful! If not for them we would have missed one of the highlights of our trip to Fiji.

In 1978 I spoke at the annual meeting of the American Bio-chemical Society in Atlanta, Georgia. Much to my surprise, the place I spoke was not an ordinary meeting room but a grand ballroom. The

Phyllis with then graduate student, Rick Harding.

Phyllis receiving the ESA Award.

Phyllis and Bert touring Japan.

huge venue filled to capacity with no empty seats, and many people were standing. There must have been over six hundred people there. Unfortunately, I came down with an intestinal bug right before the talk and was not certain whether to sit near the platform with easy stage access or near the exit, so I could bolt out if needed. I guess the adrenaline took over, and much to my relief the talk went well with many questions following.

I returned to Atlanta in 1989 to receive the Dal Nogare Award in Chromatography from the Chromatography Forum of Delaware Valley. It was a celebration, and I felt honored to be the first woman to earn this prestigious award. When I attended these meetings, I had one problem the men did not have—what to wear. I wanted to look professional at the meeting and yet dress up for the evening dinner held in my honor. I finally decided I would wear a suit and tailored shirt for the meeting. I brought a small suitcase with me and then went to the ladies' room to change into my prettiest dress for the evening. The men only had to decide on which tie to wear.

Being one of the keynote speakers at another biochemistry meeting held in New Orleans, I arrived at my hotel hot and tired. The lobby was jammed with people attending the meeting all clamoring for a room. While waiting in line, I watched as the front desk staff turned away a number of people who, I assumed, did not have reservations.

When it came my turn, I confidently stepped up to the registration window and handed the young man on duty my reservation card, only to have him quickly reply, "I'm sorry. Your reservation was to have started yesterday and we could not hold your room. We're completely sold out and have nothing else available."

And indeed, I had made my reservation for the wrong day. All of the hotels were full, and I didn't know what to do. I realized it was my fault and told him I understood.

As I turned away dejectedly, I must have looked very sad because he stopped and said quietly, "Wait a few minutes. Maybe I can manage something."

After what seemed like an eternity, he motioned me back to the counter and gave me a key. They had subdivided a huge suite on the top floor and given me one-half of it. It was gorgeous with a magnificent view, and they only charged me the price of a regular room! I lived in luxury for the rest of the week. I was relieved to have such nice accommodations—in fact any accommodations. I did not know any women there that I could call upon when I needed a bed. The men could bunk together when these issues arose.

In the early 1980s I spoke at the Washington Chromatography Discussion Group. Bert and I were delighted to visit Washington, DC, where we spent the first few years of our married life. It was a large meeting with several hundred people in attendance. The evening began with dinner followed immediately by my talk. A few minutes before I was to begin, we all filtered from the dining room into the presentation hall. Much to the dismay of the organizers, we found the slide projector had disappeared. Fortunately, I had not yet loaded it with my slides. Those in charge quickly scurried around to find that one or locate another one but were unsuccessful. Finally, they asked me if I could give the presentation without slides, which I did. Halfway through my talk, they found another projector, and I loaded up my slides and continued.

After I spoke and finished answering questions, a man came to me and complimented me on my talk, but continued on by saying, "I really liked your talk much better without the slides!" and then he disappeared.

I got a chuckle out of that one and many more to follow.

I received many calls asking for help relating to HPLC, most wanting free advice, and depending on who was asking and what it was for, I was happy to oblige. I later found out my colleagues had consulting services and charged for the time taken from their own research. So when a friend of a friend called me and wanted a short course over the telephone on specific analyses, I asked him why he needed this information. He told me he was a consultant to a company and needed this information to advise them. In other words, he wanted me to provide this information free of charge, and he was going to sell that information to his client. I said I would be very glad to consult with him for a fee or split the fee he would be receiving. He became very upset with me and hung up in a huff. I never heard from him again. I had no regrets in how I handled that phone call. I was glad to be done with him.

One late afternoon I received a call from a man with the investment firm of Shearson, Lehman, and Hutton. When I first spoke to him, I thought he was trying to sell me some stocks, and I was very abrupt and hung up. He called back to tell me he was not trying to sell me anything, but inviting me to speak at a small symposium in New York. Every year, Shearson invited several experts to speak to a group of their brokers gathered from all over the country. They invited speakers based on the field in which these stockbrokers specialized. That year the area of interest was chemical instrumentation, and he asked me to speak on the advances in analytical separations made possible by chromatographic instrumentation. The company paid extremely well and covered all travel expenses. In addition, I tried to talk Shearson into getting me two tickets to *Phantom of the Opera*, the top musical on Broadway at the time, but I was unsuccessful. A good try but I finally went to see the play the next spring when we were at an HPLC meeting in New York.

When we were first married, Bert did all the traveling. In the Navy he was sent all over the country and for the long trips went by airplane. After his Navy service he went to Europe to have molds made for his plastic business. He used to fly on Friday nights to Portugal, work all day, and then take a plane home on Sunday. Monday, he was back in the office. I will never forget when he came home so excited from flying on a jet plane! Before that he flew only on prop planes (short for propeller). Since I had never flown, I was not impressed; it made no difference to me. He was disappointed I was not as excited as he.

After Bert sold his business in 1973, we traveled a lot either because I attended a conference or spoke somewhere. The first HPLC meeting I attended was in Amsterdam in 1978. As an eager novice at an international conference, I attended all the sessions and affairs planned for the participants. I was thrilled when one of the luminaries stood up after my talk and said it was the most elegant paper on exciting, innovative research presented at the symposium. Such compliments were rare, and it helped me gain recognition on the international scene. We loved Amsterdam and were delighted they held several meetings there during the time I was an active chromatographer.

After a couple of meetings, my colleagues grew to know Bert. Whenever my friend Cal Giddings attended a conference too, he would call and ask, "Is Bert with you?" If I answered no, Cal would always say, "Why didn't you bring him?" If Bert was there, Cal would suggest going out to dinner together. When I attended a meeting abroad, I would tell Bert about the meeting, and he decided whether he wanted to come with me. The only time he decided not to come was to Baden-Baden, Germany. After I returned and told him how lovely Baden-Baden was, he regretted his decision.

I had heard of the wonderful springs in Baden-Baden better

known as baths, and since I was a spa junkie, I wanted to experience them for myself. It took a day or so to locate them on a back street, so I decided to take Wednesday afternoon off from the meetings and go for a visit. Before you entered the baths, steps needed to be taken. I met another American woman as I entered the building, and we went through the procedures together. Finally, we came to the baths and looked into the pool. Much to our surprise and dismay, we found both men and women in the pool—stark naked! We looked at each other, clearly both wondering if we should go in, and we agreed that we paid for the experience, and no one else seemed to mind so in we went. After soaking in the pool, they wrapped us in a blanket for a short rest.

They did not realize what a good sleeper I was! An hour and a half later, I woke up with a start and realized I was late for a VIP reception. I quickly dressed, dashed to my hotel, threw on my best dress, and rushed over to the reception. I made my appearance toward the end of the reception, pink and rested in a light print dress. In contrast, all the men and women in the symposium looked gray and tired. Being the only woman speaker, my absence was noted, and they asked where I had been. When I told them the Baden-Baden Spa, the locals started to laugh. I had visited the baths the only day it was co-ed. I had not read the spa's sign, written in German, which explained the policy. From then on, at every meeting they teased me about my afternoon off at the baths. Baden-Baden was lovely—where time stood still. The ladies dressed up to stroll with their dogs down the lovely tree-lined walk and the McDonald's was hidden from sight for their huge sign was not allowed.

At a meeting in Munich, a music-loving colleague from Israel and I found it was opera season. We quickly bought tickets for two operas, *The Magic Flute* and *Andre Chenier*. Although we dressed up in our best clothes, I felt like a country bumpkin at the Opera House. The natives were dressed to the hilt in their formal best. In addition, my friend with his heavy Israeli accent explained to me the stories, which were sung in Italian and French. How international!

At a later meeting in Amsterdam, my colleague and I bought tickets for a concert given at the *Concertgebouw*, world-renowned for the hall's outstanding acoustics. We ate dinner in a lovely little restaurant, which we thought was next to the concert hall. Much to our surprise, the concert for which we had tickets was not next door but in another hall several blocks away. By hustling we arrived just in time to take our seats on the stage behind the first violins. What a treat! We could almost read their music along with the violinists.

Amsterdam was the setting of several international conferences. At another conference we had a lovely dinner at a local restaurant with a group of chromatographers. During our walk back to the hotel, we began discussing the art of writing. One of the chromatographers said that after he wrote an article, he would put it in a drawer for a week. Then he would take it out and correct it as he reread it. Everyone took turns sharing their unique method of writing and proofing their work.

My friend Cal leaned towards me and said quietly, "Once I write a paper, I never change a word."

And that was true; he did not. Cal wrote beautifully with nary an extra word or phrase in his crystal clear English. I think he wrote and rewrote everything in his mind, and when he finally put down his thoughts on paper they were perfect. He once asked me to modify an article he wrote to include more examples, but I found it impossible to insert any new ideas or any reason to change a word.

When a friend who taught in Amsterdam heard I was going to be in Europe, he invited me to speak to the chemistry department of his university. He was an outstanding chromatographer, and I wondered why he wanted me to speak to his students. His reply to that question was similar to that of John Knox from University of Edinburgh. "We have many women graduate students in chemistry. However, we have no women faculty members and have never had a woman speaker in our seminar series. I want our female students to see that a woman can be a successful scientist, especially an analytical chemist." I met with those students after my talk, and I thoroughly enjoyed the experience.

Over dinner, I told my friend that the Netherlands intrigued me because as a child, I had loved the story of *Hans Brinker and the Silver Skates*. I added that I wanted to skate on Amsterdam's frozen canals in winter. My friend replied mischievously that if my next visit to Amsterdam was in winter, he would arrange for me to skate there—but I had to use wooden skates, just like Hans Brinker. I laughingly accepted but made sure I was not in Holland in the winter.

After my visit to Amsterdam, Bert and I planned to meet in Rome and then fly together to Milan. Our daughter Judy would pick us up and take us to Trieste where she was staying. Because Bert could not come with me to Amsterdam, he was flying in from New York. I arrived in Rome at the stated time, knowing I had a short time before Bert's flight would arrive. I sat down near the gate where we were to board our next flight to wait for him, and waited, and waited, and waited. Since there were no cell phones at that time, I had no way of contacting him. I really began to get worried; the time for our plane to depart for Milan was approaching and no Bert. At the last minute he came running into the airport. His plane had arrived at the international airport, and he waited there for me. Then he finally realized that there were two airports in Rome, and I was at the national airport. Luckily, he arrived just in time for us to catch our plane, and Judy happily met us in Milan.

We had a wonderful trip to Europe in the summer of 1985. I spoke at the twenty-first International Chromatography Symposium in Oslo, Norway, the first week of June. The HPLC '85 meeting in Edinburgh was the first week in July and unexpectedly, I was asked to chair the fifth Eastern European Symposium on Chromatography in Budapest, Hungary, the week after the Oslo meeting. There was no point in coming back to the USA between meetings, so Bert and I arranged for a little vacation, partly in Florence, where we had yet to spend much time, and partly in Portugal, where Bert had gone many times for business, but never took the time to see the sights.

Unfortunately, Bert needed a hernia operation two weeks before we left. I didn't know whether to cancel our whole trip or at least the first part of it. The surgeon was a friend of ours, and when I asked him whether Bert should or could travel, he said, "Sure, but don't let him lift any bags for six weeks. You'll have to lift them off the baggage carousel." He continued, "He can recuperate in Europe just as well as at home."

So off we went, and he made a complete recovery overseas.

We did take it easy in Oslo but were still able to participate in the events of the symposium. By the time we arrived in Budapest, Bert had regained his energy, and we explored the sights. Since Hungary was still behind the Iron Curtain; it was an interesting experience. There was very little merchandise in the stores, and we were warned not to change any money if asked to do so. You could feel the oppression and the desperation of the people. I was surprised at how large a delegation arrived from Russia, and when I remarked about this to one of my friends at the meeting, he replied quietly, "How many of the Russians participated in any discussion?"

I realized only a select few seemed to be involved. My friend then said there was a small group of scientists; many of the larger groups were KGB personnel sent to prevent the scientists from defecting while out of the country.

Bert and I attended a lovely and lush party in the hills of Budapest one evening. Beautiful roses decorated the rooms, the vodka flowed, and the caviar kept coming. I later learned the party was given by the head of the Russian delegation, also a KGB member, who siphoned off a little of the money she was allotted for the delegates for her personal expenses. It was quite a bash.

The first afternoon we were in Budapest we took a cruise on the Danube. I had expected to see the beautiful Blue Danube, but the river was anything but blue—more like a dirty brownish green. However, we had a great time. There was a class of young children onboard. We could not speak Hungarian, which they found funny, and they howled when we tried to pronounce the names of the landmark buildings as we passed them, no matter how hard they tried to teach us.

Budapest, called the City of Spas, is famous for its baths. We finally found the main one in an ancient building. While I went into the baths, Bert waited for me in the large entrance hall. After I finished I tried to find Bert, and—much to my consternation—I became lost in the many halls of that large building. I could not ask directions because no one spoke English. After what seemed to be an eternity, I finally found Bert. Was I glad to see him! I thought I was lost forever.

In the hotel we saw an announcement that the Broadway musical *Cats* was playing in Budapest. Since neither Bert nor I had seen the play at home, we bought tickets. It never occurred to us that not only would the dialogue be in Hungarian, but so was the program. However, it was an amazing production, said to be the best in Europe, and we discovered that *Cats* is a musical you can enjoy watching the action and the dancing, without understanding the language.

My adventures in Japan started while still in graduate school. Bert came home one day in 1967 and said he had to go to Japan and Hong Kong on business. At first he was going alone, but the more I thought about it, the more I wanted to go with him. I did not know when I would have another opportunity to see that part of the world. He was thinking the same thing, so we arranged to go together. My advisor, John Edwards, had been telling me I should take a vacation and that I had been working too hard for too long. So, I went to see John and told him I was taking some time off.

"Where are you going?" he asked.

Casually I said, "Around the world."

At first he didn't react, but suddenly he said, "Around the world?"

Then I explained that Bert had to go to Hong Kong and Japan, and I was going with him. Since Bert's brother and his wife were in Spain at the time, we decided to fly to the Far East via California but come home via Spain so we could visit Norman and his wife, Trude.

Since I was going to be in Japan, John wanted me to visit a professor in Kyoto who might be helpful to me. John immediately sent him a letter and a meeting date was arranged. After Bert finished his business in Tokyo, we took the super express train (SEX) to Kyoto. We took a taxi to the university, and the professor met Bert and me at the gate. After a brief introduction Bert and I arranged to meet at a set time. Then Bert went off sightseeing, and I went into the confines of the university. The professor and I had a very good visit talking about my research, with him interjecting some helpful comments. Then he handed me off to one of his assistants.

Finally, after meeting many people in the department—most of whom spoke little English—and drinking innumerable cups of tea, the assistant escorted me back to the gate to meet Bert. We waited and waited but no Bert. Since it was the era before cell phones, I had no way of contacting him. My anxiety quietly increased as the minutes passed. After what seemed to be an eternity, during which I was sure I would never see Bert or my children again, my guide suddenly remembered there was more than one gate to the university, and maybe Bert was waiting at another. Sure enough, there he was, just as worried and anxious as I. What a relief to see each other again!

We did not get back to the Pacific Rim for many years. In 1993 my friend Kiyokatsu Jinno invited me to give the plenary talk at a Japanese HPLC symposium in Kyoto. Bert and I were delighted to have the opportunity to go back to Japan. By now I had more contacts. I was hoping to meet Katsyuki Nakano, a Japanese scientist who had spent a year in the 1980s working in my laboratory, along with the professor who translated my books into Japanese. I wrote to both of them, telling them of my plans and our arrival date. Kiyokatsu also notified several companies that I would be in Japan, and because of this they invited me to give seminars to their analytical staff.

I boned up on Japanese culture, so we would not make any faux pas. Because neither of us wanted to eat any raw fish, I wrote in advance telling everyone we were vegetarians. Unfortunately, our first night in Kyoto they had a dinner in our honor, at which they served delicious-looking cooked shrimp and fish, which we could not eat since they had specially arranged a vegetarian dinner for us. Were we ever sorry! This happened several times during our visit.

Our host and his wife were most gracious and showed us the highlights of Kyoto, Toyohashi, and other interesting cities. I agonized about what to wear at the Symposium, especially what shoes to wear. I wanted to look smart and professional, but still, I knew I would have to walk a lot. For the day of my presentation, I finally settled on some shoes that were not particularly attractive but were very comfortable. However, I didn't need to worry. At the place where I gave my talk, I had to take off my shoes and wear slippers they provided. All that worry for nothing!

In talking to Jinno, I asked why he had invited me. He replied that in all the years he was active in the Japanese HPLC symposia, he knew of only one female speaker; she was quite formidable and did not relate well to the female graduate students. He thought they needed a role model, and I could be that person. Jinno arranged for me to meet with the graduate students and the women at the meeting for lunch. It was an interesting experience. The women all hungered for information on succeeding in analytical chemistry but also feared being too proactive on their own behalf.

Because the organizers of the symposium could only give me a limited honorarium, Jinno arranged for me to speak at several companies to cover my expenses while in Japan. At the end of each morning talk, a group from the company took us out to lunch; if it was an afternoon presentation, dinner. At the end of the meal, they discreetly slipped me an envelope containing money to pay me for my talk. In this way my expenses were more than adequately covered.

At Shiseido, a large company that manufactured pharmaceuticals and all types of cosmetics, their management also handed me a large bag with an array of their beauty products. Since I have never been a shopper, I had no idea of the value of these products. In addition, since the bag was very heavy, I blithely gave away everything along the way before we returned home.

When I mentioned this to a friend back in the states, she looked at me in amazement. "Do you know how much Shiseido products cost?" she asked. "Go check them out."

The next time I was in a department store I did, only to discover that I had given away at least $500 worth of lotions, perfumes, etc.! They were top of the line products.

Poor Bert, he sat through all my talks in Japan. Luckily, I gave a different talk at each place, so it wasn't quite as boring as it could have been. At one of the lunches, we went to a traditional Japanese restaurant and sat on cushions on the floor. Unfortunately, Bert had a knee problem, but he gamely sat with his legs crossed underneath him. He must have been in agony, but he never complained.

Another Japanese friend took us out to dinner. When we started out in the morning, it was a lovely day, but in the afternoon storm clouds appeared. By late afternoon the heavens opened up. The winds howled and the rain came down in sheets. Our friend disappeared for a few minutes and reappeared with a large umbrella, which was useless in the wild wind. We then went to a teahouse for tea. At the time we did not understand that our friend was stalling; he had a dinner reservation and had to keep us busy until the restaurant opened. He suggested going shopping, but we were not interested, so he took us to see the huge Buddha in the middle of town. We stood in the wind and rain admiring the Buddha, but politely rejected his repeated suggestion of climbing a steep flight of grass-covered stairs to inspect it closer. He then hired a taxicab and showed us the beach nearby.

When the waves broke over the sea wall, Bert whispered to me, "If the water comes over the wall again, let's run."

Of course, there wasn't any place to go, as the other side of the road was a steep hill. Our friend sat impassively and didn't seem to worry at all about the howling winds and smashing waves.

Finally, we went to the restaurant, another lovely, traditional Japanese restaurant. By the time we finished dinner and caught the train to Tokyo, the streets and train stations were empty. We were in the midst of a genuine typhoon and we—those crazy Americans—were the only ones out in it!

In Japan we saw more statues of Buddha than I knew existed. In every city we visited, our hosts took us to see the famous statues and shrines. I was glad I packed good walking shoes, or I would not have survived. I admired the way my host arranged our stay in Japan and seamlessly handed us from host to host in different cities. The symposium at which I was initially speaking was in Kyoto, but I also spoke in Osaka, Toyohashi, and Tokyo.

Katsyuki Nakano hosted us in Osaka. A scientist at the Perfect Liberty Health Organization, I was thrilled to see him again, after having spent a year with him in the lab. He and his lovely wife took us sightseeing, and we walked what seemed like miles. Finally, they took us to their apartment. By American standards it was very small, and the four of us just about fit in the living room. We later learned it was unusual to be invited into a Japanese home and felt honored they extended us such warm hospitality.

In Kyoto we met the University of Kyoto professor who had translated my first two books into Japanese. We all shared a laugh when I recounted to him how many years earlier, the publisher had sent me the Japanese proofs to read, but the only words I understood were my first and last names, which were in English. The professor was engaging and very knowledgeable. We had a very enjoyable visit, and I was sorry we could not spend more time with him.

Of all the cities, Bert and I liked Kyoto the best. It had an old world charm that had not been destroyed by either the war or modern progress, and the Buddha in the center of the city was especially beautiful.

In the mid-1980s I spoke at a conference held by the Russian Academy of Sciences in Yalta. At that time to enter and travel in Russia behind the Iron Curtain, you had to have a travel plan. It was a little scary to go there, but Bert and I decided we would go. We really wanted to see the part of the world from where our ancestors came. I immediately wrote the chairperson at the Russian Academy of Sciences asking for a travel plan but did not receive one. Then I received a call from someone at the Russian Academy of Sciences asking why I was not coming. I carefully explained that we needed a travel plan to get our visas. I waited patiently and still no plan.

One day while in my office, I was paged because I had a call from Moscow. Again, I explained what I needed. They misinterpreted my reluctance to come as being due to the low honorarium, and then they raised the ante. This pattern continued for several weeks, and each time they raised the payment a little more. One of the last offers was airline tickets for two to Yalta, expenses for four days in Yalta and then a week in Moscow. The final offer included someone to meet us at the Moscow International Airport and escort us to the national airport where we would catch our plane to Yalta.

The last part of the offer was very important because there were planes to Yalta only two or three times each week, and if you were held up for any reason in the International Airport, you could miss your connection and possibly miss the conference. However, they still did not send the travel plans and I reluctantly cancelled our plans to go to Russia a week before the meeting. The plans finally arrived two days before the meeting, but it was too late to go. I am not sure what caused the problem. Although my name was on the program, I never showed. Maybe some of the conference officials were saying, "Just like a woman, so unreliable." I'll never know.

In the early 90s, I received an unexpected telephone call. The World Bank was sponsoring a trip to China to help the Chinese government upgrade a technical school into a graduate program in chemistry. I was asked to take charge of the project. They offered me first-class, round-trip airfare to China and would cover all expenses for six weeks. When I told Bert about it, he was very excited and wanted to go; it was a chance to see China at the minimal cost of his airfare to China. However, after discussing the pros and cons of such an undertaking, we decided not to go. The school was out in the country, miles from a city. I worried about the language barrier. I would be on my own, not with a group, and the medical facilities were minimal.

It was fortunate that we did not go. Bert had a heart attack during the period we would have been there, and without modern medicine he probably would not have survived.

CHAPTER 8

Life in Israel

~

I met Professor Eli Grushka from Hebrew University at a meeting in Houston in the early 1970s.

I stood near the buffet table at the reception when he came to me, introduced himself, and said, "I wondered what you were like. I've read your papers and they are very interesting!"

That started a wonderful friendship leading Bert and me to spend four semesters in Jerusalem. Eli and I were a great team; he was a physical chemist and I, with my biological and organic background, did some exciting research, which resulted in strong collaboration and a number of papers together. In fact, Eli and I co-authored some of my best articles.

However, his initial statement did not surprise me at the time because everyone at the meeting was wondering about that woman who had invaded their private domain: an all-white boys club. Moreover, I gave a strange talk about applying their technique to problems they neither understood nor cared to understand. The fields of biology, biochemistry, and medicine were outside their line of vision, and unless you discussed the theoretical aspects of chromatography or its instrumentation, these men were not interested—which was lucky for me. I had this whole area of applying chromatography to real-life problems all to myself.

It took them at least ten years to realize the gold mine in this area of research. Now the articles in analytical and chromatography journals are mainly on applications and there are few articles on instrumentation or theory. For example, without HPLC the advances in gene sequencing would not have occurred. Of course, the development of computers was also vital to the tremendous advances we had made in medical research since the 1970s. However, it amazes me when I read current articles; there is little mention of the breakthroughs we made in the 1970s. There is nary a reference to the body of work that made the current research possible. Research done before computers seemed to have dropped off the map. No one goes to the library anymore to see research published prior to computers.

After the meeting I continued corresponding with Eli, and in 1977, when I was eligible for a sabbatical, I wrote to him about the possibility of going to Jerusalem for a semester. He put the wheels in motion, and in the fall of 1979, Bert and I headed for Jerusalem. At the time, Hebrew University had so many professors visiting from all over the world that they had a special office devoted to taking care of these professors' housing arrangements.

We arrived in Jerusalem on a very hot day, which is common for late August. A representative of the university met us at the gate. He helped us through customs and drove us to our apartment. The apartment was in a graduate student complex on the fourth or fifth floor. We carried the luggage for our six-month stay up the curved staircase. Our driver had the key to the apartment, but when he tried to open the door it would not work. He and Bert struggled with the lock for about twenty minutes, and after visiting the main office, the driver found a key that finally worked.

To say the apartment was minimally furnished was an understatement. After looking around to see if we needed anything, our driver left. Why Bert locked the door after him I'll never know, but he did. It did not occur to him that the key was not reliable, and when we decided to go out and take a walk, we could not get out. We were locked in with no telephone or means of communication with the outside. Since it was vacation time and all the students were gone, we were alone in the building—no one could hear our calls for help. What a feeling of helplessness. Luckily, Bert is technically inclined, and after working on the lock for over an hour, he finally was able to open the door. What a relief.

We found the office and told the secretary of our plight, and she said she would notify the maintenance man but did not know when he would get to us. As we went back to our apartment building, we saw someone waving to us. It was Donna Grushka, Eli's wife. She came over to see if we had settled in and if there was anything she could do for us. As we told her our story, we decided that this is not the apartment for us, and we would go to the King David Hotel until we found a more suitable residence. Luckily, Donna was there and graciously helped transport us to the hotel. She also knew of an apartment in their building that might be available. It was just wonderful to be in the King David, with its luxurious furnishings and a lovely shower after our long trip. We were rewarded at night when the sky was lit up with a full moon hanging over the walls of the old city. What a magnificent sight! It was a sign of good things to come.

The next day, Donna called to say there was an apartment in their building we could sublease, and within a couple of days, we arranged to move in. It was a lovely apartment. We were there only a few hours when the phone rang; people from Providence called to invite us to their daughter's wedding. They heard we were in Jerusalem, and none of their friends or family could come to her wedding. Would we be their Providence representatives for this happy occasion?

"Of course," we said and asked, "When is the wedding?"

"Tonight at seven." And they gave us the address.

After rummaging through our luggage to find suitably festive clothes to wear, we called a cab, and arrived at the hotel a few minutes before the wedding began. Much to our surprise, the only people there were the bride and groom, their parents, and the rabbi! Everyone else in Israel knew that weddings do not start at the time on the invitation, and we hung out with the families until it grew dark and the guests arrived.

Since Orthodox weddings are performed outside under the stars, we all trouped up to the roof for the ceremony then back indoors for the reception. What a celebration, with the men dancing and singing on one side of the room and the women on the other. We were introduced to the Israeli scene with a bang! After the wedding there were seven days of partying, but we begged off for many of the festivities. There was too much to do settling into our new home.

Eli was in Europe when we arrived, and upon his return he and I started on our research project. Early on Eli discovered the power of computers and insisted Bert and I rent one in Israel. Bert, who had some exposure to them when he was in business, took to using it like a duck to water. I was a little slower, and my learning curve was steeper, but little by little I chipped away at it. By the time we left Israel in late December, I felt somewhat computer-literate. Bert had conquered DOS and I, WordPerfect.

That first semester in Israel was very productive in our research together. We collaborated on one of my best papers, which was published soon after in the journal *Analytical Chemistry*. However, not all was work, and every afternoon Bert and I took time off to explore Jerusalem. I think you could be there for years and not see all the historical sites going back centuries. We lived down the road from the amazing Israeli Museum, where you could spend hours and hardly see any of it. In addition to the displays, they held concerts and lectures there, and had a lovely little café. I bought a book on walking tours in Jerusalem, and many an afternoon we followed the paths outlined in the book. With each walk we learned a little more about the long and exciting history of the city. The place we loved best was the Old City, where much history was made. We spent many hours behind its walls, wandering in the alleys, and exploring the backways.

To the outer world, Israel—and in particular Jerusalem—was

often painted as a dangerous place. However, Bert and I felt safer going into the heart of Jerusalem in the evening than we did going to downtown Providence or New York at night. The streets overflowed with people enjoying coffee at one of the many outdoor cafes or shopping at the open stores. It never occurred to us not to go out. From time-to-time we received telephone calls from our children urging us to come home. They felt it was too dangerous; but of course we had no intention of leaving.

Within weeks of our arrival in Israel, there was an international meeting on chromatography in Lausanne, Switzerland. I was presenting a paper, as was Eli. Bert and Donna decided not to go with us. By now the boys who ran the meetings were used to me and accepted my papers for presentation. Even so, I was still not fully accepted, in that I was not asked to be on the scientific committee or chair a session. However, in general they tolerated my presence and let me tag along. The meeting went well, but I still hadn't learned how important it was to mingle during the meetings (and only go to some of the sessions) or sit in the bar where all the important decisions were made about the next meeting. It took several years before I became a full-fledged member of the boys' club.

Lausanne was a lovely town, and the highlight of the visit was our trip up a mountain in a gondola. I had not known that Eli had a phobia about heights, and I watched him turn more and more green the farther we went up the mountain. I was afraid we were going to lose him, but he did survive the ordeal. There at the end of the ride was the amazing sight of hang gliders, men literally jumping off the side of the mountain, which blew our minds.

Bert and I went through the usual adjustments of living in a foreign country: first we fell in love with it then we missed our comfortable life in the United States. We felt a little homesick and lonesome for our family. Finally, we adjusted to the new culture with its pros and cons. Life in Israel was not easy in 1979. Although for the most part the people spoke English, the telephone book and the street signs were in Hebrew, as were most of the labels on foods in the grocery stores.

Since Bert did a lot of the shopping while I was at work, he learned to ask questions in his fundamental Hebrew and always found some kind woman to shepherd him through the store. At the bank he had a difficult time trying to procure a safe deposit box for us. Since the woman in charge spoke no English and Bert did not speak enough Hebrew to make her understand what he wanted, they finally found they could communicate in Yiddish and Bert accomplished his business.

Each semester in Israel was different. Although we had been to Israel on short visits in 1963 as tourists and in 1973 for a conference, living in Jerusalem was very different. In 1979 we had to learn to live like natives without speaking their language. Since I knew very little Hebrew, and Bert had minimal command of the language, it was a struggle to do even the simplest transactions. Riding the bus was an adventure but trying to rent a car even more so. After several meetings with the man in charge of the rental cars, we finally procured an old large station wagon, which was great when we had company or to move pieces of furniture we bought to make our apartment more livable. The only problem with this vehicle was parking in the small spaces planned for the much smaller cars owned by most Israelis.

Having a car made life much easier, and with Bert driving, we scooted around Jerusalem. I only drove on Shabbat (Saturday) because there was supposed to be no driving on the Sabbath, and the streets were empty. Israelis are very aggressive, impatient drivers known to drive with their horns. Because the car had a stick shift and the city had many hills, I was nervous behind the wheel during the week. Bert loved the challenge and drove like an Israeli.

During the first rainfall in the fall, the driving was treacherous. When the dust and oil combined with the water, it was as slippery as an icy December day in Rhode Island, and cars slid all over the roads. At first Bert could not believe that the Israelis did not want to drive because it was raining, but he soon realized the danger.

There were few movie houses in Jerusalem, so when I heard that an excellent movie was coming to the Jerusalem theatre, I planned to go. Because I was unfamiliar with the fall holidays, several times Bert and I arrived at the theatre to find it closed because of some minor holiday. Finally, I found a date when the movie was playing, and we went over early to be certain we would get tickets. As Bert was parking the car, I went into the theatre to buy our tickets. When I asked for the tickets, the person selling them asked, "Are you sure you want to go to a Spanish movie with Hebrew subtitles?" I thanked her and headed back to Bert and the car. Jerusalem has a diverse and cosmopolitan population! We saw the movie when we returned to Rhode Island.

Besides doing research with Eli, I taught a course (in English, of course) on the uses of HPLC in biochemistry and gave several talks in Israel at Hebrew University and the Weitzman Institute. Bert kept busy by working with the computer and studying at an ulpan, a school offering an intensive course in learning to converse in Hebrew. He also kept up his physical fitness program by jogging up and down the Jerusalem hills. He was quite a model for our Israeli friends.

Bert and I were very fortunate that the Grushka family adopted us. They invited us to their family parties, as well as all holiday celebrations. We even went with them on vacation when they went up to a kibbutz on the Galilee over the Sukkoth holidays. Something that surprised us was the number of religious holidays celebrated in the fall. It seemed like every time we turned around, there was another holiday—holidays that were celebrated only in the temples in the USA. The fall semester did not seriously start until sometime in October, after the last of the holidays were over. But they didn't have time off for Thanksgiving and Christmas the way we do here.

The sabbatical was a great success, for not only Eli and me professionally but also personally for Bert and me. So when I received an invitation to come back to Israel in 1983 for a semester as a University Fellow, we happily accepted. We were able to get a university apartment in the same building. This apartment was not as well furnished as the one we sublet previously, but with a little fixing up we made it quite livable. Bert and I truly cherished our time in Israel, and both of us were thrilled to return when I received a Fulbright Fellowship in 1987 and then a Lady Davis Fellowship in 1994.

In 1987 we arrived before the semester started, so that our son, daughter-in-law, and their children could visit us before the grandkids started back to school. It was very hot during their visit, so we arranged to see other parts of Israel. We stayed in several kibbutzim—one on the Sea of Galilee, one near the Dead Sea, and one on the Mediterranean that had a waterpark next door. Many of the kibbutzim had guesthouses for tourists, and it was fun seeing Israel from different places. We especially loved seeing Israel through the children's eyes, and they were very good travelers. During the 1987 stay we had many visitors from Rhode Island who were tourists on short visits. We loved to hear news from home, and they enjoyed being in a typical Israeli home.

In 1994 we went to Israel in February for the spring semester. Our other sabbaticals in Israel had been in the fall semesters, and we wanted to be there for Passover. Also, there were so many holidays in the fall that it seemed as if the school term would never start. We had not counted on the numerous holidays after Passover! It is a wonder the Israelis can compete with students from other countries with all their holidays. We also did not realize how cold Jerusalem could be in the winter. We rented a university-owned apartment, and when we arrived in the middle of February, there was only one not-very-warm blanket in the apartment. We planned to buy additional blankets, but for the first couple of nights, before we could go shopping, we were freezing. We were so cold that we slept fully clothed in one twin bed to keep warm. Fortunately, we met our neighbors, a nice young couple, who lent us extra comforters when they heard our plight.

The lab was no better, and I wore every piece of warm clothing I brought with me—layers and layers of clothes. In addition to being cold, the school semester started poorly with all the staff going on strike. However, since I was on a Lady Davis Fellowship, I had to teach my course despite the strike. What an eerie feeling it was to walk on a deserted campus and enter an almost empty building. My students dutifully came. Although I was very uncomfortable, I taught my course in the cold, empty building. On top of this I developed laryngitis and for a couple of lectures I croaked, which really bothered the students.

It was bad enough they had to listen to my lecture in English, not their native language, but also with this maddening voice in an empty, cold building. Altogether, it did not make for the best teaching experience. However, after Passover the strike was settled, the sun shone, and the buildings warmed up, so it ended on a better note than it started.

Most weekends we packed a lunch and went with the Grushkas for a hike or picnic in some scenic place. With them we went from Metula near the Lebanese border, to the Golan Heights, and to the Dead Sea. We enjoyed lovely picnics in the forests and the caves outside of Jerusalem that a tourist would never know of. On Sukkot, the entire Grushka family—grandparents, children, and grandchildren—packed up and went to a kibbutz near the Sea of Galilee, Ayelet Hashachar. There, we went swimming in the sea and sunbathed on its shores. On one picnic near Metula, Bert accidently locked his keys in the car with the motor running. Since we were out in east nowhere without a nearby AAA and of course without a cell phone in those days, I panicked. But everyone sprang into action with heated discussions about the best ways to open the car and retrieve the keys.

Members of the Israeli army were there, as well as police officers patrolling the area and a good number of tourists and picnickers—but the one who saved the day and snaked his way in to get the keys was Eli's brother, Avi. He expertly picked the lock and voila, the door was open. We shut off the motor and grabbed the keys. Everyone was involved and a loud cheer erupted when the door was finally unlocked. We were very careful with the keys after that.

Chanukah was fun in Israel, and it was exciting to see everyone celebrating the holiday that only a small percentage of the population back in the States acknowledge. We went into the Old City to see the chief rabbi, dressed in his white fur hat and resplendent white outfit, light the huge menorah at the Western Wall. We were also invited to parties at the homes of friends. Everyone brought their own menorahs *(chanukiot)* and placed them on a table. If it was later in the week and five or six candles were lit in each menorah, the light was so bright it lit up the room. At one home there were homemade jelly doughnuts, and at another the doughnuts were fresh from the local bakery. When the holiday began, the lines were long to get the doughnuts fresh out of the oven. More than latkes, Israelis used the doughnut as a symbol of the oil that unexpectedly lasted eight days.

Because there had been a female prime minister of Israel and there were several women on the faculty in the chemistry department, I thought Israel would be more egalitarian. I had looked forward to bonding with female colleagues. However, I was disappointed. Although the women chemists were very polite, they showed no interest in women's issues, and I hardly got to know them, no matter how hard I tried. Whether they were not interested in the issue or had fought their way up the ladder and wanted to spend all their energy on their research and their careers, I'll never know because I could not get close enough to them to find out. So again, it was life with the boys.

CHAPTER 9

On the Home Front

When Bert was a student at URI in the 1930s, there was one female member of the chemistry faculty, Dr. Margaret Parks. She held a PhD in chemistry from Columbia University, and her husband was a chemistry faculty member who subsequently became the department chair. As a woman, Dr. Parks was permitted to teach only the freshman courses or any courses involving the nurses (i.e., the women.) Men taught all the other courses. Even though she was highly trained and a fine chemist, she could not teach any of the upper level chemistry courses. Since she and her husband retired years before I worked there, I did not get to know her. In fact, I do not remember knowing another woman chemist after leaving Simmons College, where all our chemistry professors were women.

When I was a student at Brown, no women were on the chemistry faculty—no women role models. In the early 1980s this lack of women came to the attention of the NIH. After a site visit to Brown, the NIH officials inquired why there were no women professors. The answer was that no female candidates for recent positions had come up to Brown's standards. The officials replied that since they had women graduate students and were receiving funds from the NIH, they had better search harder and find some good women candidates, or the NIH funding would be withdrawn. Interestingly, after that they found an excellent female candidate for the position, with a PhD from Harvard. Coincidentally, the next person they hired was a woman with a PhD from Columbia. Isn't it funny how quickly highly qualified candidates appeared? Both women were successful. Unfortunately for the Brown Chemistry Department, one of the women became a dean in the graduate school and the other was lured away by another university, so the process of finding good women for the chemistry faculty had to begin again.

It never occurred to me that once I received my PhD and started working, I would be in an almost all-male society. In the pharmacology section at Brown, outside of the secretary or occasional technician, I was the only female on the staff. Therefore, I never went out to lunch with the boys. In fact, when the faculty members took a visiting speaker out to lunch, I was not even invited. They went to the University Club, which discriminated against women. For lunch, women could only come in via the back door.

Even though many more women were graduating with PhDs, and although I campaigned tirelessly to get other women on the faculty, I was unsuccessful. Except for the secretaries, I was the only woman on staff in the chemistry department at URI, so every day was life with the boys. Committee meetings I ran, both within the department and in the university, were highly popular—not because of me, but because I always served cookies and a beverage. It was part of my housewifely training. The men did not bother with such social niceties.

In addition, because I was the token woman from the physical sciences, whenever URI had to show diversity, I was appointed to a committee or board and the administration could say: *See, we have women scientists!* This tokenism was hard on me. I had the same load of teaching, research, grant writing, and other duties to complete as the men, but in addition I had to represent the women in science. Therefore, I was delighted when we hired a lovely young woman as an analytical chemist. On paper, her record was stellar and she seemed as wholesome as apple pie! However, were we wrong! Everything was fine for about a year, and then she started to unravel. At first it was flunking a good number of her students, and then complaints of harassment both about her and from her began too. Finally, we realized that she was mentally unstable. She would make outlandish accusations, so everyone feared being alone with her. No one wanted to take her classes because she failed everyone and graduate students did not want to work with her because she made extremely unreasonable demands on them. Then we gradually heard she had previously had similar problems. It was nearly a full two years of terror before she moved on. Our wholesome, pink-cheeked faculty member had turned into a Frankenstein.

After that bad experience the staff was a little leery of hiring another female faculty member. Luckily, a very bright couple came our way through the Gordon Research Conferences, a Rhode Island-based, independent organization that holds conferences to promote the sharing of ideas within the biological, chemical, and physical sciences. Both husband and wife became faculty members. Interestingly, the woman was the outside person, the star with an international reputation, and her husband ran the lab and did the majority of the teaching.

They were childless, and it never occurred to us that they would have children. With all her accomplishments we assumed her childbearing years were over. However, right before I retired she announced she was pregnant. Although it was a very difficult pregnancy, she did not miss a beat and worked until the baby was born.

The department decided we should give her a baby shower. A couple of months before the baby was due, Bert and I hosted a co-ed shower at our home. It was the first time most of the men had ever been to a baby shower, and we all had a great time. Everyone thought that this baby boy would be an only child, but to everyone's surprise two years later, he had a little brother. Moreover, two years after that, I heard that twin girls completed the family.

When I began my teaching career, I not only had to deal with the male professors and administrators, but I also did not know how male graduate students would feel about having a female advisor. Fortunately, the times were beginning to change, and without exception I felt accepted and respected by all of the graduate students that I had the pleasure of teaching.

At URI I initially inherited the two male students from Dr. Rosie and added two new graduate students—one male and one female. In my first graduate course on separations in the fall of 1973, I had six very bright students: five male and one female. Since I had never taught an analytical course and had not put together a syllabus, I did not know where to begin.

My friend Jim Fasching, chair of the search committee that hired me said, "Have them clean up your lab, and then assign each a project."

That was good advice and as soon as I was able to obtain instruments, each student began their research.

After the first year my lab group usually consisted of half males and half females—not intentionally; it just happened. I taught an international crew with students from all over the world. The senior graduate students monitored the incoming ones, and after the first couple of years, my lab operated smoothly. However, each group had its own personality, and some years they were a contentious lot. They fought over everything, especially instrument time, as I did not have enough instruments to let each one have his or her own.

More importantly, since we were pioneers in the field of HPLC, we were developing instrumental procedures as we went along. There were times when the results were not reproducible. One day Ante, one of my senior graduate students, was literally sitting on my doorstep when I arrived at work. He was visibly upset.

"My instrument isn't working. I will never finish. I can't use it. I want to use the Waters' instrument." (The favorite instrument in the lab.)

I sat him down and said, "Ante, that instrument you are using was engineered to work. It is your job to find out why it isn't working." I then discussed possible variables he could change and sent him packing. I did not hear from him or see him (because he worked in the lab mainly at night) for several weeks. In fact, I was worried that he had gone back home to Yugoslavia. However, several weeks later an exuberant Ante was waiting for me with reams of paper when I came in.

"Look!" he said, "Look at the great results I got last week," and he showed me the results of his successful experiments.

Problem solved, at least for the present. In due time Ante graduated and for many years held a responsible position in Paris, as head of the analytical laboratories of a very large cosmetics corporation.

One of the funnier moments was when Ante, who spoke seven languages and was very cosmopolitan, was complaining to me about his lack of social life. I asked him why he did not take out one of the cute girls he had met the previous semester in one of his labs.

"Oh, Dr. Brown," he said, "How can I take out a girl from Cranston?" mimicking the local accent perfectly. After graduation he married a lovely Parisian doctor who had an impeccable French accent.

At each national meeting where my students spoke, I always took them out for a celebration dinner after we had all given our talks. Early on, at a PittCon meeting in Cleveland, we went to a small French restaurant recommended by the chairperson of our session. Much to our delight Ante started to converse in French with our waiter and then with the owner of the restaurant. That night, we not only had delicious food, but also superb service!

To make a cohesive group and foster bonding among my students, each year I had a holiday party right before Christmas break, and we also celebrated everyone's birthday, either with a luncheon, or if that was not possible, at least with a birthday cake. The events I enjoyed most were usually the graduation parties at my house. I threw a party the night before graduation or a brunch graduation morning. Many of the students' families would attend, giving me the chance to meet them.

One memorable graduation party was for Pam. She was from a large, New York Italian family, and they all came—parents, sisters, brothers, grandparents, and I think some aunts, uncles, and cousins too. She was one of the first in her family to go to college and definitely the first to get a doctorate. In addition, she had a job waiting for her at one of the large instrument companies where she had worked for a couple of summers. Her yearly starting salary was to be higher than her father had ever earned in a year. One sister living in California was very upset that she could not be at the graduation.

On the phone, she said to her family, "Everyone is going to be there but me. This is more important than going to a wedding. You can have more than one wedding, but you can only get one PhD!"

The family got together and sent her a ticket to come to Rhode Island for the graduation. They were a wonderful family and the celebration was heartwarming.

Another graduation party was for Christina from Scotland. Her father had earned his PhD, after he retired from his job in the ship building industry, and both her brothers had PhDs. Her mother came over from Scotland, and one of her brothers came to the graduation in his kilt. Since he was very tall and handsome—and the only person at graduation in Scottish dress—I could easily spot him in the crowd.

I had been at URI for several weeks when the two new graduate students started working with me. They could not have been more different. Rick was accepted with the provision he complete some missing coursework. He had graduated from a Bible College, which had few of the courses required for a BS in chemistry. He had taken a few of the required courses at Providence College, but he did not have the solid background in either the math or the chemistry courses needed for a graduate degree. Everyone in the department was delighted he chose to work for me. I heard later that behind my back faculty members were saying it was a good fit because he would not last and neither would I, given my one-year contract. However, we both surprised them.

Rick was amazing. He was like a sponge, soaking up the necessary material. He was a very hard worker and loved learning. Occasionally, he hit a bad spot and was discouraged. The remaining graduate students and I would encourage him, and he pushed through the rough patches. When things looked insurmountable, he would go home to his parents and do some manual labor on their farm. After a few days he was back, refreshed and ready to do battle again.

One day he came to me and said, "Dr. Brown, I don't write very well. Will you help me?"

His statement about his writing was a huge understatement. He was a very poor writer, but took criticism well and was willing to learn. When he did not agree with my comments, he would argue with me politely, which were good discussions.

After a couple of years, he said to me one morning, "Dr. Brown, are you sick?"

"No," I said.

"Are you sure you are not sick?" he asked again.

"Why, Rick? Do I look green?" I asked.

"No," he replied, "but you returned the last paper I wrote with no red ink on it."

I always corrected papers with a pen with red ink. I smiled and said, "Rick, there's nothing to change in that paper. It is very well written."

As it turned out, Rick became one of the best writers of all my graduate students. Initially, he applied to get a master's degree, but he did so well we all convinced him to stay on and work for his PhD. His thesis was excellent. He went on to that very prestigious NSF post-doctoral position under Dr. John Knox at the University of Edinburgh.

When Rick started working for me, Joy asked if she could join my group. If ever there were opposites, it was Joy and Rick. Whereas Rick had a poor background and his credentials on paper did not look promising, Joy was a Regent Scholar from New York, with a strong math and chemistry background. She was a star and the faculty was delighted she had come to URI. Many of the professors wanted her to work for them and were more than a little upset when she chose me.

She was extremely bright; everything came easily to her. In fact, she had been so successful throughout her schooling that she thought she knew it all, and she definitely thought she knew more than I did. Since I was new to leading a research group, her attitude had me feeling very insecure. I noticed that only she called me by first name and challenged me at every turn. I finally put my foot down. I told her that students should address me as Professor Brown or Dr. Brown, and that she would earn the right to call me by my first name when she received her PhD.

Joy did a brilliant piece of research for her PhD thesis. However, instead of applying the procedure she had developed to a variety of uses, she stopped after applying it to two compounds. I urged her to follow it up with a number of other applications, but she refused. She said she had enough research for her thesis and was finished. She wrote up two papers and then relaxed until she got her degree. Rick, on the other hand, even when he had enough material for a thesis, continued working, and he wrote many more articles than were required for his thesis.

Unlike Joy, most of my other female students never felt their research was finished. They seemed to feel the research was never good enough, and they had to do more before they could write it up. When I finally convinced them their research was finished and they had to write up their results, they only wrote a minimum number of articles, whereas the men stretched the material and produced many papers. No matter how I tried to build up the women's self-esteem, I could rarely instill in them the self-confidence the men had.

Besides Joy, Kate was an exception to this. She was the youngest of six children and the only girl. Early on, she learned to compete and hold her own with her brothers. When I had the opportunity to collaborate with a colleague at Waters Associates, I asked Kate if she wanted this project for her research. The man in charge of the project was brilliant but had a difficult personality. I gave her all the facts and told her it was her decision. She thought the research was exciting and went to work on it. Several times she almost quit, but in the end she stuck it out. She did a great piece of research, and she published many articles on it.

One day I walked into the lab and heard swearing that would make a sailor blush. Ann, a graduate student who came to me from the corporate world, was my first student to write her thesis on a computer. For several years she had worked on the development of desktop computers while at Hewlett Packard. She certainly knew how these new-fangled contraptions worked, but somehow she did not save her material properly. She lost her thesis that she had so patiently typed into the computer. It took me hours to calm her down enough so she could start putting it together again. Ann was very feisty and did not accept criticism gracefully. She disagreed with what I taught and how I taught. Five years after she graduated, Ann was the one who called to thank me for teaching her how to give a talk. That was a highlight of my teaching career!

No matter how hard I worked with my students, I was not always successful. One year I had two male students who were not meant to be chemists. One was a playboy, the son of a wealthy corporate executive. He was very bright, but studying was not his top priority. Getting him to keep his nose to the grindstone was difficult, but he finally did just enough work to get a master's degree in chemistry. He charmed his way into a job at one of the big instrument companies where he rose in the business side of the company. He finally ended up going into business—exactly what his father had always wanted him to do.

The other student had a drinking problem that I did not recognize until it was very serious. My other graduate students banded together to tell me that he was drinking heavily in the lab at night. He became dangerous to himself and to the other students. He left URI, and I later learned that he found religion, sobered up, and finished his degree at another school. I never heard from him again.

From Pennsylvania came Mary, a lovely, young graduate student. When applying for admission, her parents brought her to Rhode Island to make sure that this would be a suitable environment for their daughter. They fell in love with the beaches and seashore, and it did not take them long to buy a summer cottage in Narragansett.

Mary was a good student and fun to have in my group. However, she was so shy that giving a seminar was torture for her. Gradually, with practice, she became able to give presentations, and by the time she graduated, she presented very good seminars. After graduation she went to work for a large instrument company in Massachusetts. A couple of years later she called me and said, "You'll never believe it, Dr. Brown, but I just got back from a trip to Europe. I gave a seminar in a different country every day!"

I heard her speak at a national meeting soon after, and she wowed her audience. I was so proud of her. A number of years later, she called me to tell me she was promoted to the regional sales manager for the corporation. Excitedly she exclaimed, "I'm now in charge of fourteen men." Over the years, I heard reports about her great work and that she was widely respected in the field.

Another student from Pennsylvania was a young man who came to URI with a very strong background in math and chemistry. He was very creative and a fine experimentalist. I only had one problem with him: he did not want to leave. He loved Rhode Island, he loved working in the lab, and he loved being his own boss. I finally had to put my foot down and make him finish. Luckily, he met a lovely young woman who was also a graduate student in chemistry, and together they graduated and moved to Pennsylvania where they both obtained good jobs.

A friend at Northeastern sent a wonderful young woman to apply for the graduate program in chemistry. She was a hard working student, but I never thought she really wanted to be a chemist. After graduation she went to California where she found a job; however, a short time later, I received an announcement that she had married. I was honored and flattered when she later told me that she named her first child, Felicia, after me. She had several more children, and I do not believe she ever went back into chemistry.

In the middle of the 1990s, I was chairperson of graduate admissions in chemistry. I was amazed when I saw the list of graduate student applicants in chemistry. Of the 500 names on the list, 495 were from China; only five were American. I showed the list to the president of the university. He in turn revealed the list at a meeting of university presidents because it augured poorly for the future of science in the United States. We later found out URI was not unique; our graduate schools were filled with Chinese graduate students who eventually took their abilities and training back to China. Subsequently, the United States was already suffering from a lack of trained scientists, and it will most likely get worse. The brain drain had started in earnest. All we could do was fill our graduate classes with Chinese students, which made it difficult for the undergraduates. Graduate students were teaching assistants in the undergrad courses, and although these students were competent, their lack of English skills made it frustrating for everyone.

I had my share of Asian students, starting with Bob from Taiwan, the other student inherited from Dr. Rosie. Bob was a good student and nice young man. For a few years he would send me a gift on the anniversary of his graduation in thanks for taking him on as a student. The presents were unnecessary but a nice reminder of his time as my student. After about a dozen years, the presents gradually stopped, but I heard through the chromatography grapevine that he had done very well as a professor in Taiwan.

In the chemistry department, I had a Chinese colleague. He and I taught several courses together, as well as collaborated on some research. Over the years Bert and I became close friends with him and his wife. After they adopted a little boy from Taiwan, we stopped by their house one night and met their son, who was now about two years old. He took one look at me, cried "Grandma!" and ran into my arms. From then on I had a delightful and rambunctious Chinese grandson who gave his parents quite a run for their money. These quiet, scholarly people did not quite know what hit them when their son grew up into a hippy musician. He finally settled down and is now a dedicated public school teacher.

Another student from mainland China went by the name Sheila. She was very mysterious, and my students decided that she was in the equivalent of the Chinese secret service. She was a brilliant student but a loner who never bonded with any of the other students. Unbeknownst to me, she was working on a master's degree in computer science at the same time she was enrolled as a graduate student in chemistry. She was smart enough to pull this off. I never did learn what her background was or where she went after she left URI.

My Chinese connection was strongest with Mr. Yi. As do many foreign students and scientists, Mr. Yi wrote asking if he could travel to URI to work with me. I answered him that I would be glad to have him, if he had funding for his stay. Letters went back and forth, and then one day I received a telephone call that Mr. Yi had arrived. What a surprise! I had lunch with him, and despite his lack of English, learned that during the revolution in China, he was forced to leave school and work the fields in the countryside. He never finished his doctorate and wanted to complete his work here and receive the equivalent of a PhD in chemistry.

I was taken aback. There was no precedence for accomplishing this. I also had made no provision for instrumentation or desk space for a visiting scientist, and I did not know where to put him. My students came to my rescue; they rearranged the furniture, made space for Mr. Yi, and scheduled him on instrument time. After a year Mr. Yi announced he had to go back to China and had written up his research. I was pleasantly surprised at his excellent English in the papers because I thought his comprehension of the English language was poor. After a colleague at URI reviewed the papers, Mr. Yi submitted his papers for consideration, and subsequently, they were published.

Several months after Mr. Yi's research was published, I happened to read an article written by a friend of mine in Missouri. It sounded similar to Mr. Yi's findings. For one paper Mr. Yi had copied pages of results from my friend. I started investigating more and found he had copied results word-for-word from a paper by a German chemist. I was appalled! I had to write both authors to acknowledge and apologize for his plagiarism then write to the journals to publish my apology. I also called my friend in Missouri and told him what had happened. He thought it was funny and was not upset.

That was not the case with my German colleague who was not amused at all. In addition, my friend told me that Mr. Yi had called him in January and said he wanted to leave me and spend the rest of the year in his laboratory, but my friend told him he did not have space for him. I wrote Mr. Yi to tell him that copying from another paper was entirely unacceptable, but he never answered me.

Several years later, a very bright student from China enrolled as a graduate student, and lo and behold, it was Mr. Yi's daughter. Although she was an excellent student, she only planned to get her master's degree. In the end she did stay on to get her PhD. While she was here, her mother, a biochemist, came to visit, and I had the pleasure of getting to know her. I never spoke with either about what had transpired with Mr. Yi.

I had a number of Asian students sent to me by former students or by colleagues. Yong-Nam came with a master's degree from Northeastern. When I saw a friend who had previously taught Yong-Nam, I asked why Yong-Nam did not stay at Northeastern for a doctorate, and my friend's response was guarded and somewhat vague. I gathered Yong-Nam was difficult to work with. In addition, since his field was separations, he wanted to work with me. He was very bright and had a solid foundation in math and chemistry, so at first I had no trouble with him. However, when he wrote up his thesis, I did not agree with some of his conclusions and did not want them published as written. Yong-Nam became difficult, defiant, and argumentative while stubbornly refusing to rewrite his thesis, as his committee and I had requested. Soon afterwards, he packed up and left for Korea. About six months later I received a copy of our article in a Korean chemical journal with my name credited alongside his. Since everything was written in Korean except our names, I never found out what it said, but I assume he submitted the paper just as he had written it. I never heard from him again.

We rarely received applications from Japanese students. Their own universities were excellent, and I had heard that they did not feel the need to get their graduate education in the United States. However, I received a letter from Katsyuki Nakano, a Japanese scientist at the Perfect Liberty Organization. He wanted to spend a year in my laboratory learning to use HPLC to assay for nucleic acid constituents. While he was here, we learned that the Perfect Liberty Organization was a religious group with its own education, health, and scientific facilities. Since he failed to inform me when he was arriving, he suddenly appeared on my doorstep, and we had to scurry to find housing for him. After he had settled in a motel in Narragansett, about five miles from the university, one of my graduate students came to me partly laughing and partly distraught. He asked me if I knew anything about the motel. Before I could answer, he blurted out, "Did you know it was the center for prostitution and drugs in the area?"

This gentle, religious man had landed in a den of iniquity in our bucolic beachfront town. We quickly scoured the area and found lodging that was more suitable for my Japanese colleague. He fit very well into my group, and the other grad students adopted him and protected him for the year he was with me. We had a happy reunion when I visited him in his hometown of Osaka eleven years later.

Given that my focus in chemistry was more about application than theory, I worked closely with industry, which provided me a good source of graduate students. Some quit work and attended school full-time working towards their degrees, while others attended school part-time. I found all of these young people were great students. Having been in industry, they realized the importance of their degree and did not waste time; they focused on their work. Most of these students were either from Waters, the manufacturer of chromatography and other analytical instrumentation, or Pfizer, a pharmaceutical company.

With several of the other professors in the chemistry department at URI, we started a joint program with Pfizer offering a master's degree in analytical chemistry. Every semester we taught a graduate course down at Pfizer. The class lasted three hours, one day a week. Pfizer allowed the students to attend an hour and a half of the class on company time and an hour and a half after work. Every semester, following a set sequence determined jointly by Pfizer and URI, various professors taught a course. I helped set up the program and taught two of the courses.

Since we started at three o'clock in the afternoon, before the normal workday was over, parking was difficult. However, one of my students who worked at Pfizer realized this, and he came out and watched for someone to leave the parking lot. He then stood in the space until I arrived, so I did not have to walk very far. He also carried my rather heavy briefcase up to the lecture room. The first time I taught there, I was amazed to find an auditorium filled with about a hundred students. Although I was unprepared for such a large class, I worked my way through it. The first semester, Pfizer put out delicious cookies and coffee for us for our fifteen-minute break. I told everyone at URI about this added bonus teaching in industry, but the next semester there were no cookies. The Pfizer employees all found out about the cookies and ate the cookies as soon as they were set out. And that ended our little tea party. Over the years some of my best graduate students came from those classes, and it was a joy to teach them and watch them advance in the industry.

Although I did not teach a formal class at Waters, I knew many of the staff there. When someone voiced an interest in continuing their education, many times he or she was referred to me, and URI started to have a good reputation for continuing education in chemistry. There are many unforeseen advantages of having students from the corporate world. At an HPLC conference in San Francisco, a group of us wanted to attend a reception held a few miles out of town. For some reason we could not get transportation to get there. One of my Waters' students told me to wait a few minutes, headed out, and then returned in a white, stretch limousine. We all climbed in and sped away. Where he got it or how, I will never know. I asked no questions, and it was fun while it lasted.

I encouraged all of my students to participate in national meetings, and preparing talks was part of my curriculum. Most of my students became very good at speaking before groups. I always told them that even if they were the most outstanding scientists, it meant nothing if they could not explain the material clearly—both orally and in writing. The old days of a scientist working alone in a lab were over. We had to be able to communicate with other scientists.

I was so naïve when I started teaching at URI that I did not realize my résumé was far superior to most of the chemistry faculty members. I also did not know I earned less than most of them. I had no idea how to negotiate a higher salary or better teaching hours. Whatever I was handed, I obediently and graciously accepted. Only many years later did I find out that I had received the largest NIH grant ever given to URI. No one informed me that I could trade teaching time for research time. Moreover, I spoke nationally and internationally more frequently than any of my colleagues. I later learned that I could have requested startup money to set up my lab. At present, new professors get sizeable funds to start their research. If I had not borrowed instruments from the large manufacturers, it would have been nearly impossible to get started. No one mentored me, and I was too naïve to ask for guidance.

One kind professor in the pharmacy school, however, came by and offered to buy supplies for me from his funds, which was a great morale booster. No one expected me to stay more than the year specified in my contract, and there were no other offers of help from the university. I did have friends in industry, including one at a company that developed and manufactured chromatography columns. He was most generous when I let him know I needed help, as were some of the others. Over the years he sent me their new columns to try. Only later did I realize that I was helping their company as much as they were supporting me, when we published our results using their equipment.

Despite my naïveté, I prospered at URI—partly because I was funded by federal funds, partly because of the support of industry, and partly because of my great group of graduate students. Over the years my credentials and authority grew—more papers, more national and international talks, and more funding. Within seven years I became a full professor with tenure at URI.

One of the advantages of attending these international meetings was that I connected with outstanding scientists who would give seminars at URI when they were in New England. They all enjoyed a weekend by the shore, and after they gave their seminars, we showed them the sights of Rhode Island. We took countless trips to show our guests the mansions in Newport, followed by dinner on the coast in the picturesque fishing village of Galilee. We developed a regular tour route that we repeated many times. My students especially benefitted from their exposure to meeting these top chromatographers in the field.

In getting to know other industry experts, I was invited to apply to the University of Georgia for a position as a professor in their chemistry department. Bert and I flew to Atlanta and rented a car to drive to Athens, where the university was located. It was hot, and the red dirt roads were dusty. After the cosmopolitan atmosphere of Atlanta, rural Georgia seemed like something out of the last century. The university was lovely, and we stayed at the home of Professor Rogers and his wife, transplanted Yankees. While the Rogerses were getting ready to host a reception in my honor later that afternoon, a young faculty member showed us around the university, especially potential housing. When our tour was over, Bert and I said to our guide that we preferred the section where the Rogerses lived.

He laughed and said that area was the Yankee ghetto.

We looked at each other and knew that this was not the place for us. Our opinion was reinforced when at the reception, we overheard faculty members discuss the plans to get rid of the only woman who was in the upper echelon of administration in the university. This was no place for a middle-aged woman from New England. Although the faculty praised my seminar, when we returned home I withdrew my name from consideration for the position.

I was excited when asked to give a seminar to the chemistry department at MIT, the most prestigious science university in the East; however, the day turned out to be a nightmare. When I arrived at MIT, I drove into their parking garage but found no empty spaces. I struggled turning my large car around to exit a garage built for small cars. I finally found a parking space on the street. I was getting flustered because I was afraid I would be late. I practically ran across the campus and arrived on time—but hot and sweaty.

After the seminar no response came from the attendees. The professors all sat stony-faced in the front two rows. The students and post doctorates did not ask a single question. *Oh dear,* I thought, *I'm a failure.*

After the seminar, when I returned to my car, I realized much to my dismay that I had locked the keys in the car. We always had a spare key hidden outside the car, but I could not find it. In a panic, I called Bert, and he gave me directions on how to find it. I was lying on the dirty road in my light lavender suit to reach it. This made me late to pick up our daughter Judy who had just finished the school year at the College of Fine Arts at Boston University. Because of her crabbiness on top of my own, we started home and missed the exit off the highway—now we were on the way to Albany, not Providence! I had bad memories of the entire day.

About ten years later, a young woman scientist at Bell Labs called me. She said I probably did not remember her, but we met when she was a graduate student at MIT and I gave a seminar.

"Oh," I said, "That was such a failure!"

"No," she protested, "That was the best seminar we had that semester. The staff even gave a cumulative exam based on it."

Surprised by her comment, I replied, "There were no questions, no interaction at all. The professors sat stone-faced and didn't say a word, nor did the students."

She replied, "That is the way it always was at our seminars. The professors wanted to appear all-knowing and the students were afraid of looking stupid or foolish in front of the staff. Afterwards, however, we had a lively discussion about the material you presented."

After a full decade, I discovered that my seminar at MIT had not been a disaster!

CHAPTER 10

The Local Boys in My Life

~

When I look back at my career, I can count the number of women role models on one hand, no less. Luckily, I went to Simmons College where the majority of the professors, even in the sciences, were women. I remember fondly Miss Ina Granara and Mrs. Florence Sargent, my chemistry professors at Simmons.

When I announced toward the end of my sophomore year that I was getting married, Mrs. Sargent said to me, "Phyllis, after your experiences in the chemistry labs, you won't have any trouble cooking. Just follow the recipes like you do instructions in the labs, and you will do fine." And she was right! Cooking never fazed me, and if I must say, I was a good cook.

At the time it did not bother me, or even occur to me that male chemists would not be met with such a sexist comment implying that I was not going to work, did not have the capacity to work, or would immediately ditch my career for love—or if I married, that I would inevitably be doing all of the cooking! Not a wife and a partner, but a housekeeper whose sole purpose was the care of the house and the man I married.

Although she was a strong advocate for women, Mrs. Sargent lived in a very different time. I understand this may have influenced her comments to me. She understood that I might not have a career, if I married so young. Perhaps she believed women's roles were so entrenched that my early marriage would preclude a professional career. However, the role model provided by my grandmother, who came from Latvia, had a strong imprint on me. In her teens she worked first as a governess for a family in Latvia then as a seamstress, first for the family and then independently once she settled in the United States. After she had several children, she ended her career as a dressmaker.

Once in the world of chemistry, I found a sole woman role model. Six years after I was entrenched in my own career, Gertrude Elion received the 1988 Nobel Prize in Medicine and Physiology for her work on chemotherapeutic agents for cancer and other diseases. I met her before she won the Nobel Prize, when she came to Brown as a guest lecturer in the pharmacology section. She was a lovely woman, brilliant, yet down to earth and very approachable. Our paths crossed many times during my working life. One time, we both attended a Gordon Conference in Plymouth, New Hampshire, not far from our vacation house on Newfound Lake. I invited her to spend an afternoon with us, and she enjoyed the peace and quiet of an afternoon by the lake. Another time, after a conference in Jerusalem, we were going to Haifa to visit a cousin, and she rode with us to visit her relatives.

Dr. Elion had a much harder path to cut than I did as young female scientists, and it was inspiring to see what she accomplished. Although she was not able to work for her PhD, she received several honorary degrees. At the Nobel Prize ceremony, when she received the award along with her co-worker George Hitchings, she was the one who gave the acceptance speech. Whenever I would get depressed about a problem with discrimination, I would think of her, and it would lift my spirits. She was a great person, a brilliant scientist, and I was glad to say she was a friend and role model. I will always be very grateful for the female role models that I did have throughout my life because most were blazing trails far steeper than my climb.

Likewise, I am hugely grateful to the men who played important roles in my life. Most offered support, encouragement, and at times, the nudge I needed to continue on my journey. In looking back, I am even somewhat grateful to the men whose goals and behavior were less noble. Their actions, likely driven by ignorance and insecurity, may have frustrated me, but they also fueled the drive within me to succeed, in spite of the roadblocks they threw in my way.

The most important man in my life was my husband, Bert. In the era when men expected their wives to stay home, run the household, take care of the children, and be at their beck and call, Bert was different. He insisted that I finish my junior and senior years in college, even after we married. Moreover, when I had tired of volunteer work and the children were in school all day, he helped me find direction and suggested that I go back to school. When I was overwhelmed with schoolwork, he encouraged me to go on by saying, "You can do it. Let me take over some of the household chores, and you take the time to study." Wherever we went, I always had my books with me, and when I had carpools or doctor appointments, out came the books to study in whatever time I had. He shared in my victories when I did well in an exam or a course and commiserated with me when I failed to master a subject.

If he had asked me even one time, "Do you have to do this?" or "Do you have to study tonight?" I probably would have given up, but he never did. He protected me from family and friends (especially my father), when they did not understand the demands on my time or why I could not go to a party, a dinner, or other social obligation. He also understood the times I was present in person, but my thoughts were on my studies. When I finally got my PhD, he was the most excited person in the audience at the graduation ceremony. He threw a great party at which we celebrated our oldest son's graduation from University of Vermont with a BS in chemistry along with my graduation. It was a swinging affair, and my mother's sisters, as well as my mother and dad, joined in the celebration with our family and friends.

Bert suggested that I return to school and get my chemistry knowledge up-to-date. Before my youngest child went to school all day, I had been very active in many volunteer organizations. Now I needed new challenges. When I voiced my concerns about what I would do with my life for the next thirty years, Bert took me seriously and helped me explore my options. We concluded that since my talents and training were in chemistry, I should enroll in some courses and get my chemistry back in working order. Neither of us mentioned getting an advanced degree, only to brush off my rusty knowledge and polish it up. My thought was that I could get a part-time job in the labs of the medical program that was opening at Brown University. The first step was to go to Brown and see if I could take a couple of chemistry courses. It never occurred to me to see what URI and the other colleges in Rhode Island or Boston offered for a part-time, returning student. In the early 1960s no continuing education programs for older or returning students who wanted to upgrade their education were available, especially in the sciences. Chemistry changed more in the previous twenty years than in the one hundred years prior.

It took me six months to gather the courage to visit Brown, ask about courses, and finally make an appointment with Dr. Joseph Bunnett, head of the chemistry department. I always thought that by having a wife who was a feminist, it helped Dr. Bunnett to see the potential within me. He gave me the opportunity and encouragement to return to school eighteen years after graduation and tackle the more sophisticated concepts of chemistry. He suggested that I audit an undergraduate course and see how well I could do. He did this on his own without consulting either the graduate school or chemistry faculty. However, he informed the professor teaching the physical chemistry course of my presence, so that I could take the exams.

Why I did not quit then, I will never know. I was so rusty and physical chemistry had never been a high spot in my life or my best course. Nevertheless, with Bert and Dr. Bunnett cheering me on, it all fell into place, and I earned a B on the final. The next year Dr. Bunnett encouraged me to take a couple of courses, which I did.

Bert was my mentor, my cheerleader, and my supporter. And I needed all of his support to succeed. However, if it had not been for Joe Bunnett, I never would have cracked the barrier that existed at Brown for returning students. He alone took a chance on me—without the faculty or university approval—and he had the courage to take me on as a graduate student. Back in those days, he could have lost his job by not following Brown's required protocols. He took a gamble on me, and we both won when I returned to school and received my PhD. When I had to choose a research advisor, I asked to join his group, and he accepted me.

An interesting man, Joe Bunnett was Germanic, demanding, authoritarian, a perfectionist, and was never one to be warm and fuzzy. He did not tolerate sloppiness or any insubordination. That said, if you were on his team, you always knew where you stood; he supported you and was a wonderful mentor. He tolerated no foolishness, tardiness, or absences. If you played by his rules, you had a great experience.

I remembered one post-doctoral student who was not used to this type of structured environment, and he strained at the bit. He aggravated Joe by working all night, and in the morning when Joe came in, the post-doc was at his desk, reclining with his legs up, drinking coffee, and preparing to go home to sleep. Joe was irritated because he could not control this night owl. The young man did not fit into Joe's vision of his group, but he produced such good science that Joe had to grin and bear it. We all heaved a sigh of relief when the student left, and Joe could rule his fiefdom more easily. Joe and Sarah, his wife, were about my age and had three boys. The elder two were my sons' ages.

I was dismayed when Joe told me he was leaving for the position at UCSC, but I was happy for him and his family, too. His departure brought a new boy into my life: Dr. John Edwards, and we hit it off from the start. I had already taken his inorganic chemistry course and although I struggled with it, passed it with a mediocre B. John was a wonderful teacher: clear, concise, and well organized. He was an even more brilliant researcher. Although a perfectionist, he was very kind, supportive, and an amazing advisor. He came up with an interesting project for me and gave me great freedom in my research, during which I mastered several analytical techniques, most importantly chromatography and several spectroscopic techniques. The ability to use these techniques was the basis of my transition to analytical chemistry, which helped me start my job in pharmacology and led to my career at URI as an analytical chemist. How strange the route of my life has been. If someone had told me about my journey beforehand, I would have assumed that person was crazy.

John guided me with a firm hand in the right direction toward completing my PhD in chemistry, and our friendship with John and his wife, Ruth, was an extra bonus for Bert and me. For years after we moved to Saunderstown, whenever there was a full moon coming up, we would call John and Ruth to come down and watch the moon coming up over the bay. As we drank our wine and ate our cheese and crackers, we would enjoy the magnificent sight from our living room.

After I got my PhD, the bottom dropped out of the chemistry market, and there were few jobs available in the chemical field. I preemptively took the clinical laboratory exams and became a nationally certified clinical chemist, in case the job market did not pick up, but becoming a clinical chemist was not my career of choice. Once I graduated, it was John who reassured me that I should be prepared for an opportunity when it arose, and sure enough it was John who suggested me for a chemist opening in the newly developed pharmacology section at Brown University—and before I knew it, I had the job.

Another man came into my life, a well-known pharmacologist, who came to Brown to head this new department. He wanted me to synthesize some radioactive purine and pyrimidine analogs with hopes of using them in studies of the chemotherapy treatment of cancer. When I explained that the reproducibility of 15-20 percent was not acceptable, this man told me I did not understand biochemistry and those results were fine in the biochemical realm.

One day, however, he came back from a conference having leased an instrument called a nucleic acid analyzer. Whether he may have thought assigning the machine to me would stymie my work and frustrate me or he was merely giving me busy work that no one else wanted, I was up to the challenge. While I was both exhausted and exhilarated over the next three months, the research and the resulting paper, the first of many, launched me on my defining path as a published expert on the applications of the HPLC instrument.

After publication of that article, and subsequent ones on other aspects of the research, this man turned on me. He would be alternately nice, then caustically critical. He criticized my writing and my research and disapproved of my accepting speaking invitations. I never knew when he was going to approve of my work or me—or when he was going to attack me. He was starting to undermine my confidence, both personally and in my research. My work environment kept getting worse, and many days I ended up in tears. Fortunately, I applied for the position at URI and was offered the job, but at a substantial decrease in salary.

My two saviors at URI were Dr. Leon Goodman, head of the department, and Dr. James Fasching, chair of the search committee. I remained good friends with both throughout their lives. Leon came from California to head the chemistry department at URI and build it up. He was a little older than I. He had been a fine researcher and had an enviable CV. He was wise beyond his years and a good administrator. He guided me in the new territory that was URI and encouraged me to write grant proposals. I submitted proposals to NIH and NSF, as well as any small fund I could find that might be interested in my research. I knew nothing of the politics of funding of proposals, but was wildly optimistic. Leon encouraged me, guided me, and critiqued my proposals. I do not think I would have lasted at URI without his help, and he was instrumental in getting me an appointment on the tenure track after the first year.

Jim Fasching was a recent newcomer from MIT. A farm boy from North Dakota, he had done well in graduate school and came to URI to strengthen the analytical chemistry division. He and I hit it off from the first time we met, and he showed me the ropes of survival, both at URI and in the analytical field. Jim was a big man with bright-blue eyes that seemed to twinkle whenever he wanted something, like money from one of my grants for computer equipment. Jim was one of the first researchers I knew to see the advantages of computers. Before anyone else, he said our future was in computerization, and he pushed me to learn as much as I could about computers. At first, I was reluctant to step into the computer age, but Jim was right and computers opened the way for the future.

Jim and I collaborated on many projects and I called him my partner in crime and chemistry. Because of him, I started going to PittCon, and he encouraged me to take my graduate students there. Money was tight, but we always scraped together enough to bring our students with us. After the first year, it was a goal of all my students to get enough research done to submit an abstract to the conference. It was a great incentive for them.

Over time, Bert and I became good friends with Jim and his wife, Diane—a friendship that has lasted through Jim's struggle with Parkinson's disease and Bert's with Alzheimer's.

Dr. Douglas Rosie was another influence on my career. It was Doug's position I took over when I joined URI, and thankfully, he decided he enjoyed being a full-time administrator, so I stayed past my yearlong contract. Although at the time, I did not realize that with my experience, reputation, and credentials, I could have negotiated to come in as an associate professor with tenure, so I accepted the job they offered. I came in on a one-year contract, and I stayed for twenty-eight years.

I had met Doug back in the sixties, when I was at Brown. At URI he ran a short summer course in gas chromatography, which I took. Since I was the only woman in the class, he was sure I was a dilettante, and he gave me a hard time. Many years later when I was a successful chromatographer, I teased him by asking him if he still thought I was a dilettante.

Since Doug had experience leading each of the courses I was teaching in the first years at URI, I turned to him for help or direction and always received wonderful guidance. He was very good to me over the years, and because of him, I always had easy entry to the upper administration. He was a big, genial, party-loving man, and Bert and I remained good friends with him and his wife, Virginia. The analytical division was small and that strengthened our ties over the years. Bert and I, the Rosies, Faschings, and a younger member, Ken Force and his wife, Roni, had great times together. When we were younger, and the men were alive, we supported each other through thick and thin around family and professional issues. We celebrated promotions, birthdays, and other happy events in our families and provided shoulders and resources for difficult times. Later, we banded together to face Ken's early death from a rock climbing accident and gave Roni our time and attention. Whether challenges or joy, we were there for each other. We continued to meet regularly and faced the tragedies of our husbands' illnesses and subsequent deaths, calling ourselves the chemistry widows, as we moved into our older years. To this day, the chemistry widows meet regularly for lunch or dinner.

CHAPTER 11

The International Boys
in My Life

~

Over the years, I made friends with many chromatographers all over the world; almost all were male. The females at the chromatography conferences or meetings I attended were mostly the wives or mistresses of the male chromatographers. There were also the women who organized and ran the meetings, like Janet Barr, whose business was event planning. Janet did a great job in planning and organizing symposia and following up the details as to the venue, the meeting rooms, the extra events, the dinners, and trips for the spouses.

At the first international meetings I attended, the spouses received pink paper programs that listed shopping trips and other female-focused outings for the girls. One year Bert objected, but there were so few male spouses that no one paid attention to the orientation of the trips.

My first friend in the international scientific community was Dr. Csaba Horváth, a dapper man who immigrated to the United States from Hungary. When I wrote my first article on the HPLC of nucleotides, he wrote me a beautiful letter congratulating me on work well done, adding that I showed how HPLC could be used in biochemical studies. After receiving his letter, I called him to say how much it meant to me and we became good friends. My work was based on an article he wrote with Dr. Sandy Lipsky at Yale. Whereas their article used standards, I had taken the analysis several steps further and analyzed nucleotides in real samples, such as blood cells. I also proposed a novel method of identifying the peaks by a technique called the enzyme peak shift. Before the use of mass spectroscopy, it gave positive identification of the peaks for specific purine compounds. Csaba was impressed with my research.

Csaba was feisty but the wittiest speaker in the chromatography group. He always started his talks with an entertaining tidbit and accompanying slide. He had a solid education in the classic languages and used his command of Greek and Latin to liven his talks. Always immaculate, with his black hair slicked back in place, and very courtly, he sometimes had a female companion at the conferences. It took me a few years to learn that it was not Mrs. Horváth with him; she was home with the children. I never did meet her, but Csaba and his friend seemed to hit it off well. Csaba was a fine scientist and always one of the industry leaders who planned the conferences by picking the location of upcoming conferences, selecting the speakers, and choosing a theme for each conference. In 1981 he opened the conference he chaired in New York City to users of chromatography, as well as to instrumentalists and theorists. Thus, the HPLC meetings became inclusive instead of exclusive.

When my friend Georges Guiochon, who lived in France, became a full professor, all the chromatographers were there to celebrate with him. In France's academic institutions, unlike the US, once you reached full professor, you were in complete control—the ultimate authority. When I congratulated him on the accomplishment, Georges said to me, "Now I am zee Pope!"

Georges continued to be very good to me, and one of my graduate students, Ante, did post-doctoral work with Georges while in Paris. Another student, Mona, did part of her graduate work in Paris, also

under Georges' direction. And, not to forget Norman, an undergraduate who spent a year there until he went off to medical school.

Georges chaired several HPLC meetings and a series of meetings
on preparative HPLC. He was an excellent chairperson and always open
to new ideas. He was the first chair who invited me to have a discussion
and luncheon with the women at the conference and invited the first
women, besides myself, to chair a session.

At the meetings, Georges was always present with an American
woman, a chemist who worked for the government. I learned he had
a wife and two daughters in Paris, but they never came to the meetings. Eventually, he divorced his wife (or she him?). He married his
American friend and moved to the United States. With all their connections, he had no trouble finding a job. In the later years Georges rode a
motorized scooter at the exhibitions accompanying the conference. He
had contracted polio as a young man and getting around the large area
of the exhibition hall became difficult.

There were four Americans in this group of internationally re-
nowned chromatographers. The first two I met were Jack Kirkland
and Lloyd Snyder. Well-known because of their research, they wrote an
excellent textbook together on chromatography. Their book came out
about the same time as mine, and I feared mine would not sell because
of the competition. Since my book was for absolute beginners and ori-
ented toward biomedical or biochemical studies and theirs was more
in-depth on theory and instrumentation, the books were each successful in a differing target market. In addition, Jack and Lloyd had little
interest in the life sciences.

Both men were tall, six feet or more. Since they towered over most
everyone, you could easily pick them out of the crowd. Both worked
in industry: Jack at DuPont in Wilmington, Delaware and Lloyd at a
company in California. They were two straight shooters who I always
felt I could trust. Although politically savvy, they did not use politics
as a manipulative tool the way some other chromatographers did. They
taught excellent short courses at many of the meetings, which helped
sell their books. Lloyd was one of the few who brought his wife to the

meetings, if she could get away from her work, and we had many pleasant dinners with them.

Jack's wife unfortunately was ill, and so I never met her. In later years, a fellow worker at DuPont accompanied him. She was delightful, young, upbeat, and very bright, and I enjoyed her company. Eventually, they were married.

In contrast to the integrity of Jack and Lloyd, I found—much to my dismay—that I could not trust my colleague at Northeastern University. At first, I thought he was my friend and entrusted him with information regarding my research. When I was at Brown, this man sent one of his graduate students down to befriend me. Only later did I realize that the student's intent was really to spy on me and find out about my research. This became apparent when I noticed that the Northeastern professor's research was not always original, and he borrowed ideas from my research and that of other scientists while taking complete credit for the work. He liked to see which way the wind blew and be just a little ahead of it. He was a wheeler and dealer who ended up with awards he most certainly did not deserve, and then preened like a pompous peacock when awarded them.

He was round—a roly-poly little man who smirked rather than smiled. When I would encounter him, he sometimes acknowledged my presence, and other times it was as if I did not exist. When he chaired the HPLC Conference in Boston, he ignored me completely even though I volunteered to help him and was only forty miles away. Several of the old timers noticed him snubbing me and indicated that they were not surprised. If he received an article or grant proposal of mine to review, my work was always rejected; but conveniently, his research would then head in the direction that I had proposed. In later years his brown hair turned a golden color, and he tried to stay in the game, even though he was well past his prime. For years I thought I was the only one who suffered at his hands, but later found that many of his graduate students also had a difficult time with him.

Although this man won many awards, he never received any of the bigger awards that he so coveted. I luckily was successful despite his machinations, which I later learned cost me some grants—research money that would have helped me. I succeeded despite the obstacles he put in my path.

Luckily, I met Cal Giddings early in my career. As a pioneering physical chemist at the University of Utah, he proposed the theoretical basis for HPLC. He was a brilliant, meticulous theoretician whose work made possible the development of the HPLC instrumentation. It was his invitation to write for *Advances in Chromatography* that would lead me to join him, Eli Grushka, and Jack Cazes as associate editors of the series. I was affiliated with the series for almost thirty years, first as associate editor specializing in biomedical and biochemical applications, and then as editor, when Cal retired.

In contrast to the professor from Northeastern, Cal was supportive of my work and mentored me for many years. He was the person who submitted my name to the American Chemical Society (ACS) annually for ten years for the Chromatography Award and the Separations Science Award, but to no avail. I was always a top runner-up, but they had never given those awards to a woman and they were not going to start then. I won other awards, but never one from my professional society.

After the last time Cal submitted my name, he became very angry and said he was going to Washington to twist some arms. Unfortunately, shortly thereafter he was diagnosed with cancer and passed away suddenly. I realized that if the ACS did not recognize my accomplishments when Cal backed me, I did not have a chance after he was gone. He told me a number of times that my research was more original and creative than that of many of the chromatographers who received the ACS awards, and I deserved to receive one.

Cal was a Utah native and a great outdoorsman, conser-vationist, and activist. He was an ardent skier, mountain climber, and kayaker, even kayaking the Amazon River. Always in top physical shape, his face looked as if it had been carved out of the Rocky Mountains. He loved to take one afternoon off each week and invited all his graduate students and post-docs to go skiing with him. However, it made life difficult for a young post-doc from Israel who had never seen a ski slope before and was scared out of her wits. After a couple of trials, she refused to go skiing on those expeditions, even if it meant the termination of her appointment at the University of Utah. Of course she stayed on, even if skiing was not on her list of accomplishments for the year.

Cal was a gentleman in every sense of the word, a superb researcher, and a great teacher. When he died at a young age, it was a blow to me. I lost a mentor and a very good friend, and the world lost an articulate and brilliant scientist.

I do not remember where or when I met John Knox, a genial and brilliant Scotsman. John was also a big man. As a rugged sportsman, he loved the outdoors, whether it was hill walking or sailing. He and Cal were the two outstanding theorists among all the chromatographers, and they stood far above the others in the development of theory. They were competitive but in a constructive way and worked well together. In addition, John was very kind and supportive of young people in general, and I appreciated his support over the years. Bert and I enjoyed the company of John and his wife, Jo, at conferences, and we had an especially good time when HPLC 85 was in Edinburgh.

Another major member of the international group that I connected with was Dr. Kiyokatsu Jinno. I did not get to know Jinno until the late 80s. He was a delightful man who had lived in the United States for about seven years during his youth. Because he lived in the United States, Jinno spoke near perfect English. Always dressed to the nines, he looked like a model for *Esquire*. To this day he is a brilliant and active scientist and a man of great honor. Bert and I had a very good time with Jinno and his wife in Kyoto when he invited me to give a talk at that Japanese Chromatography meeting he planned and ran.

There were many more characters on the national and international chromatography stage, and I was fortunate to know many of them. They enriched my life, as well as those of my family, and I am grateful to each one of them.

CHAPTER 12

Back to the Beginning

~

We were sitting on our patio on a clear, crisp October day when Bert turned to me and said, "Phyl, I think it's time to move back to Providence. I'm not feeling well, and we should be near our doctors and nearer to our children." Our doctors were all in Providence, and we would be an hour closer to our children, who lived in Boston.

He caught me by surprise. "I don't want to go back to Providence now. I'm still teaching, and this is the place the children gather for holidays."

He persisted, "It's time to move."

Nevertheless, I was adamant, "I am not moving!" and I considered the conversation over.

A few minutes had passed when he quietly said, "I guess I'll have to move alone." After twenty-eight years, I left URI the following June.

Although I officially retired July 1, 2001, I stayed on an extra year to finish my research and see that all my students graduated. My last two PhD students, Sue and Christina, remained to help me dismantle my office, and I worked with several of my part-time master's students from Pfizer to finish their papers. URI offered me the use of my office, if I wanted to stay on, but since we were moving to Providence, I knew I would not use it much and space was at a premium in Pastore, the chemistry headquarters. In fact, the building was old and outdated when I started in 1973 and a new chemistry building was promised. Nevertheless, not until 2013—forty years later—was the new building finally on the drawing board but still not started yet. The old building—overcrowded and outmoded—was an accident waiting to happen.

I had planned to work a few more years, until I was eighty. Reluctantly, I told my department chair that I was going to retire. I had mixed feelings. Partly, I was tired and worried about Bert, but the other part of me did not want to leave the life I loved so much. URI had been my home for so many years. We had deep roots in South County, and it was incredibly beautiful. I would miss the view from our house on Narragansett Bay in all its glory: the islands, the moon rising over the bridge, the beautiful green setting, and the different animals that came to visit us. The pace was leisurely and dress casual. We had not lived in the city for almost three decades.

When I announced we were moving to Laurelmead, an independent living community in Providence, one of my colleagues asked me, "Do you know anyone there?"

I laughed and said, "About half the people."

Laurelmead sits on twenty-three acres of land with manicured green meadows in front and woodlands overlooking the Seekonk River in back. Despite its country-like setting, we were not more than ten minutes from top-notch medical facilities and fifteen minutes from downtown Providence, with its cosmopolitan center containing great restaurants, theatres, concerts, etc. Moreover, we had lived right over the border in Pawtucket, six blocks away, for the first thirty years of our married life, so we knew the area well. The children had grown up there. My oldest son, Charlie, said when he came to dinner at Laurelmead, it was like going to his wedding reception. Half the people at Laurelmead had been at his wedding and even the wedding planner lived there.

Most of all though, I would miss my work—my students who were part of my extended family, the intellectual challenge of my research, and the stimulating exchange with colleagues. I loved giving talks at international meetings and seeing if I could hold my own when questioned by the top scientists in my field, and I relished seeing graduate students grow and mature into fine scientists. I think I was most proud of their accomplishments and looked forward to seeing them present their work at national and international meetings. I would miss the travel to meetings and conferences, especially the international trips and the excitement of meeting my colleagues from all over the world.

My last big trip was in 2001, right after the festivities for my retirement. I attended an invitation-only meeting in Eindhoven, the Netherlands, held in honor of Lloyd Snyder's retirement as editor of the *Journal of Chromatography*. The HPLC 2001 conference in Maastricht followed immediately after. All my friends who were still active were there, and we enjoyed their company at the more formal dinners and informal get-togethers. It was bittersweet, as I realized this was probably the last such meeting I would attend. The field was moving so fast that if you were not working full-time, you could not keep up with current advances. In the early 1970s I went to my first chromatography meeting, which was small and intimate; now these conferences were large, international, and multidisciplinary.

Over the years there were major changes in all areas of science. The content of the papers presented went from a focus on instrumentation and theory to talks on the applications of the instrumentation to biochemical or biomedical problems. From a select exclusionary meeting to an inclusive gathering. The attendees changed from a small group of physical or analytical chemists or chemical engineers to include many scientists in the life and environmental sciences. I think my 1973 article on "HPLC in Pharmacology" in the *Advances in Chromatography* series was the first paper on applications in that series.

When I retired, the chemistry faculty threw me a retirement party. I agreed to it with two provisions: first, it must be fun and not mushy, and second, I did not want a present. I asked that any money left over from the dinner expenses go into a fund for summer fellowships for graduate students. URI had minimal funding for these types of fellowships and without financial support during the summer, it made it difficult for students to complete their research in a reasonable time.

The day of the party started with a farewell seminar. My advisor at Brown, John Edwards, gave his last talk there, and many of my former graduate students who were successfully pursuing their careers, returned to give lectures. My daughters and my best friend sat through the afternoon of talks, not understanding a word of them. At night, the Towers banquet hall in Narragansett reached capacity and overflowed with joy and laughter. The hit of the evening was a parody of *The Little Engine That Could*, which my good friend Dave Freeman, a theoretical chemist, put together with Susan, one of my last graduate students. Dave read it with gusto and had everyone in stitches.

At the end of the evening, no one wanted to go home, and groups lingered reminiscing and talking well into the night. My family was there en masse and my grandson Ezra, who was in high school at the time, had his Mohawk haircut dyed URI colors. A colleague later told me he did not like to go to retirement parties. He thought they were boring, but he had a great time at mine. Moreover, I am happy to say that a nice little fund resulted, so graduate students in the future will benefit from my retirement. To my surprise, the administration named the auditorium where I taught so many courses the Phyllis R Brown Auditorium. I hope they take the plaque with them when there is finally a new chemistry building, so future chemists can see that there was a female professor back in the dark ages of the 1970s, '80s, and '90s.

I left the party that night knowing that we were embarking on a new and very different chapter in our lives. I loved Bert even more than I did when we were young, and I never once regretted my decision to retire and return to Providence. I knew that where we were mattered far less than the fact that wherever we were, Bert and I were there together. Still, at times I quietly grieved the loss of the life we enjoyed.

When I think back to the months leading up to that day in October 2000, when Bert told me that he was not feeling well, it all seems so obvious. Bert was changing right before my eyes, and I was in complete denial.

First, Bert stopped going to the beach and complained of it being too sandy. The beach at Narragansett was lovely and barely five miles away. We had always enjoyed going there when it was just the two of us or with our children or grandchildren when they visited. He had already stopped doing yard work, so we hired a gardener—or I guess I should say gardeners, since none could do the work to Bert's standards, and we replaced each one. He also told me that he no longer wanted to carry logs in for our fireplace during the winter, so we purchased a gas insert. I should have realized something was going on when Bert returned from a day of skiing and announced that he was giving up skiing for good. He had always loved spending the day on the slopes, but at 86 years old I chalked it up to normal aging.

While I refused to see any signs of a real problem, I think Bert knew something was wrong and when he experienced problems completing tasks he had previously done with ease, he merely decided to stop doing them. While this may have relieved any fear and helplessness he felt, it did nothing to address the cause. This was true of using the computer. He had mastered the computer early on and used it to manage our financials, among other things. He was spending more and more time on the computer. Tasks that had only taken him a few minutes were now taking much longer, and he would grow frustrated and angry at himself, at the computer, and at anyone else nearby—which was most often me. We hired Susan to help with Bert's computer problems, and she eventually handled everything for us, which made everyone's life easier.

Being a scientist, you would think I would have noticed the changes in Bert, assessed the situation, and then determined the best path to proceed. However, this was not a science experiment; this was our lives. I understand now that Bert knew he was having difficulties, and that is why he insisted on moving back to Providence and into Laurelmead.

My life at Laurelmead centered on Bert and being his caregiver. It was the right move at the right time. I sank into anonymity at

Laurelmead until 2004, when I was notified that I was awarded the CSSC Csaba Horváth Medal for achievements in chromatography. I was amazed that anyone remembered me, but an old friend whom I knew from Varian, Ron Majors, nominated me. It was hard getting together a talk. I no longer had the carefully organized files that I had maintained at URI. I had difficulty finding the material I needed for the acceptance talk. For years I could put together a talk quickly and efficiently, but now it took more effort.

The meeting was at the Mohegan Sun, a gambling casino in Connecticut. My acceptance speech was not until after lunch, but I went down in the morning to hear the other talks. Much to my surprise, Charlie and Judy brought Bert for lunch, so he could be there when I received the award. A number of my friends in chemistry also came, and it was a very festive occasion. Judy and Charlie had never heard me speak, and I think they were surprised to see their mother in a completely different role. Bert, of course, had sat through many of my talks, so he knew what to expect.

In 2006, I was again surprised to learn that I was awarded the Eastern Analytical Symposium Award. The Symposium was in New Jersey, not far from the town where my youngest daughter, Elisabeth, lives with her family. Again, my first reaction was to decline the award. Bert could not travel the four or five hours it would take to drive there, and I was his sole caregiver at that time. However, the children got together and decided that Charlie and Judy would share the caregiving duties, and Charlie's wife, Liz, who had not been able to be at the CSSC award meeting, would take me down to New Jersey. When Elisabeth heard of the expedition, she, her husband, and daughter joined us for the dinner the night before the meeting. It rained hard during our drive down and back, as well as throughout the day, but it didn't bother us. We had a great time!

Many of my former graduate students came, and Sue and Christina met us the night before the meeting to help me polish my talk. In fact, they put it on the computer; for the first time, I did not use my slides. I came into the twenty-first century and used PowerPoint. Colleagues and students I had not seen in years were there, and we enjoyed our reunion. Although Bert did well with Judy and Charlie, he missed me and was glad to see me back home.

That meeting was the finale of my career. Very few people at Laurelmead knew I had a career in my former life. Many Laurelmead residents had distinguished careers and great achievements. However, you were not aware of it unless you really inquired about a person's past.

One big difference between my life at Laurelmead and my life in chemistry was in my new life, three quarters of the residents were females. When I was young, most of us married boys that were older, and since women have a longer life span, the women outlived the men. As long as Bert was alive, I did not notice the ratio as couples gravitated to other couples. However, after he died in 2008, I was increasingly in an "old crones" society and this took some getting used to.

As a widow I suddenly found myself thrust into a mainly female world and was at a loss. I did not play bridge, nor was I accustomed to lunching with the girls. I was a square peg trying to fit into a round hole. I did not have anything to talk about with the girls. I looked around and realized that women ran all the Laurelmead committees except one—the budget and finance (B&F) committee, which was the most important committee at Laurelmead—and almost all the members were men.

When it came time to apply for committee membership, I submitted my name for B&F. At first I thought nothing of not being appointed and instead served terms on the marketing and the building and grounds committees. The next year I again applied for the B&F committee with the same results. It started to bother me; why, in an organization consisting of seventy-five percent women, there was at most only one woman on this powerful committee. After the third rejection, I started inquiring and finally was appointed to that committee. The next year, I was elected to the board of directors, which is the governing body. Eventually, more women served on the B&F committee. To the surprise of the old timers here, Laurelmead did not self-destruct and is actually running quite well. In fact, it was a woman resident—a former well-known politician—who was able to negotiate a reduction in our taxes after they were unfairly increased.

Sadly, the B&F committee was the only committee to have coffee and muffins served at their meetings. For the other committee meetings, you had to buy refreshments beforehand. Why was the B&F committee the only one to have refreshments provided? Because, of course, it was the only committee comprised mostly of men. This is an all-too-familiar story.

Recently, I went to a dinner in support of a nearby hospital. I arranged for transportation to the event for myself and offered several friends a ride. As we entered the event, those who rode with me all agreed that we should sit together. I was too slow on the draw to say anything, and I foolishly went along with them. It was such a stupid thing to do.

I had been looking forward to seeing scientific colleagues that I had worked with over the years. It was also a chance to be with people outside of Laurelmead. Yet there I was at a table of all women, most of them from Laurelmead, whom I saw regularly. To make matters worse, I found myself seated between two non-Laurelmead residents, a lovely woman who, unfortunately, was very deaf and another woman who did not talk to me. Instead of the stimulating scientific conversation that I had anticipated, I was in no-man's land—literally. I was looking forward to being in mixed company or at least either talking to some men or some people outside our community. After all those years with the boys, I was delighted at the thought of spending time with them again. In addition, I understood most of the speaker's talk, whereas it went over the heads of my non-scientific female friends. Thus, there was no discussion when the speaker finished. Life with the boys spoiled me for a girls' night out.

About a year ago I received a call from the editor of the chromatography journal *LCGC*. She asked if a young chemist could interview me by phone for an article in their journal. I was flattered and happily agreed to the interview. Because of the article, I heard from a number of my former graduate students. Among the nicest was an email from a student who had established and was running a successful commercial analytical laboratory. He was one of my PhD students I met through the courses I taught at Pfizer. Teachers may not make a lot of money, but communications like this are a rich reward.

People often congratulate me for always knowing where I was going in my career. They assume that I planned my path and followed it. Nonsense! That could not be further from the truth. After high school, I just wanted to get away from Providence. Boston sounded adventuresome, so I chose Simmons College because I knew my father would approve of me attending a college that was career-oriented. I changed my major from bacteriology to chemistry because I was not very good at drawing the tiny creatures under the microscope—a requirement in bacteriology. In those days we did not use photography in the lab, only drawing. It was serendipity that Bert was teaching chemistry in Boston and helped me when the going got rough in my first chemistry course at Simmons. I had always liked the sciences and math, plus it was an easy path for me to follow.

In addition, if Joe Bunnett, chairperson of the chemistry department at Brown University, had not taken me on as an experiment of sorts, I probably never would have pursued further education and continued on the community service/housewife trajectory.

Another positive influence was my advisor, John Edwards, at Brown who encouraged and supported me in my trip through academia. It was support from these men that helped me earn my PhD.

I followed the path opened to me and climbed the ladder to heights in the field that I only dreamed of. The secret was not limiting myself. Because I did not know what you could not do, I made a breakthrough in the rapid analysis of nucleotides and nucleosides. Again, it was a combination of luck and unawareness—with a little persistence thrown in—that helped me blaze a trail for the use of HPLC in the life sciences.

Also, it was sheer guts that made me send in abstracts to international meetings and get to know all the top leaders in the field. Consequently, that is how a middle-aged, Jane-come-lately, organic chemist who applied this new instrument to real world samples, was able to crack the rarified atmosphere of the club of analytical chemists who developed this instrument. No planning, only a lack of knowledge about what could not be done.

Because there were no women in the field, wonderful men who saw beyond gender mentored and helped me. These men encouraged and directed me in developing my career.

All during my career I tried to reach out and give a hand to young women thinking of entering the field or with their foot on the first rung of their professional development. I gave many talks at colleges and universities encouraging young women to become scientists. At times I felt guilty doing this in science technology engineering and math (STEM) jobs. Discrimination was still rampant and succeeding was much more difficult than in the medical and legal professions, which opened their gates to women who flowed in until at present many of those schools have about fifty percent women.

If you look at the statistics, women still have a long way to go to achieve equal representation in the scientific fields. The biological sciences attract the most women, followed by chemistry, then engineering, physics, and math. Look at the rosters at any schools with fine scientific programs. In addition, the biological clock and the race for tenure coincide, so it is difficult if a woman wants children and wants to succeed on the tenure track. At meetings I tried to meet as many bright young women as possible, either singly or in groups, and provide them positive reinforcement. I continued to press the chairs of these conferences to have women chair sessions or give talks to increase their exposure. In addition, I encouraged the women to submit abstracts to sessions at these meetings or write up and submit their papers for publication.

Women sometimes feel that their research is not good enough, not perfect for publication. The only way the scientific community can get to know you is by your publications and talks. Unfortunately, many women are not as assertive as men are in presenting themselves. If women are aggressive they are often labeled pushy, whereas aggression has a positive connotation when describing men. As an editor for the *Advances in Chromatography* series, I actively recruited women to

The name of the students are (left to right): Elmo Resende, Nick Bell, Jim Treubig, Tom McNabb, Christina Robb, Scott Huffman, Massy Rajabzadeh, John Seelinbinder, Sheila Zhifang Jiang, Sue Geldart and Lisa Shaner.

write articles for inclusion. Sometimes it was like pulling teeth to get manuscripts from them. On the other hand, men pursued me to submit articles for the series.

I think and hope things are changing and women are making their way up the ladder of success. By playing on sports teams, women are learning how to be competitive, and we must train them to be better negotiators and how to stand up for themselves and their rights. Only time will tell how successful we have been.

I am asked regularly if I have regrets about the path I took. There were times when family celebrations and work collided, but having the flexibility of an academic career I was usually able to manage both although there were times when something had to give, like missing my oldest grandchild's high school graduation. I hope I made it up to her by being at her college graduation. I missed spending more time with Bert after his retirement, but he never complained and seemed to enjoy having some time to himself.

The many rewards of my career far outweighed my regrets. Bert and I enjoyed traveling far and wide, living in Israel and for a short time in Tasmania. We saw Europe and parts of the Middle and Far East because of my work, often with all or a portion of our expenses covered, which made it all the sweeter. We made many international friends and experienced their countries differently than if we had only been tourists. Those years were exciting and challenging. Bert and I grew closer because of our wonderful adventures in foreign lands. In addition, I think our marriage was richer because of my career. I was a more interesting companion because of the experiences we shared. Life was not always smooth sailing, but we both grew—individually and together.

Looking back I realize that I only made one really good decision in my life. The rest flowed from it. It was marrying Bert, who viewed me as his partner and equal long before feminism ever hit the news. He encouraged me, supported me, and was proud of my achievements in the era when—supposedly—a woman's place was in the home.

About the Author

Dr. Phyllis R. Brown, PhD

Phyllis R. Brown, PhD, Professor Emerita of Chemistry at the University of Rhode Island is credited with over two hundred articles in scientific journals and known as "the Mother of High Pressure Liquid Chromatography." She wrote five books, served as editor of many publications, was a gifted teacher and advisor to her graduate students. In retirement she dedicated herself to her husband, her many circles of friends in science and the community, and her children and their families.

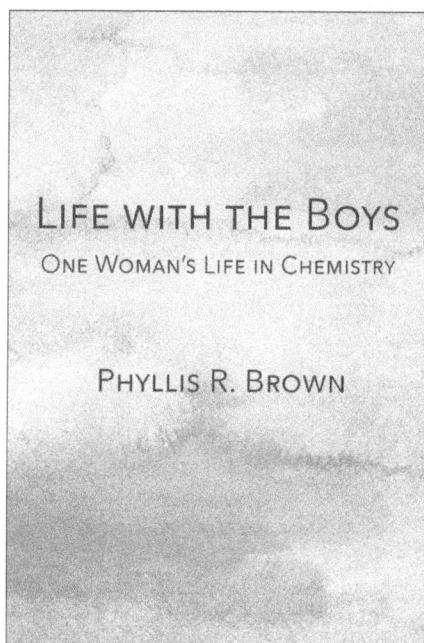

Life with the Boys
One Woman's Life in Chemistry

Phyllis R. Brown

www.phyllisrbrown.com

Publisher: SDP Publishing
Also available in ebook format

Available at all major bookstores

SDP Publishing

www.SDPPublishing.com

Contact us at: info@SDPPublishing.com

www.ingramcontent.com/pod-product-compliance
Lightning Source LLC
Chambersburg PA
CBHW022041190326
41520CB00008B/676